Rounding Up the Rhymes

A Multilevel Four-Blocks® Strategy

by

DeLinda Youngblood and Eve Hayes

Carson-Dellosa Publishing Company, Inc.
Greensboro, North Carolina

Credits

Editor
Joey Bland

Layout Design
Zoe Ranucci

Inside Illustrations
Mike Duggins

Cover Design
Annette Hollister-Papp

Cover Illustration
Lisa Olsen

ISBN 1-59441-197-2

Dedication

This book is dedicated to my grandson, Miller, with the sincere hope that he will always be surrounded by teachers who will help instill a love of books and reading.

Eve Hayes

I would like to thank my parents, Gail and Shirley Vest, for giving me the thirst for literature at a very young age; my sister, Vickie Keen, who was my perfect reading role model; my children, Randa and Zachary, who were two of the reasons for me to continue my love and excitement of children's literature; and last, but not least, my husband and buddy, Randy, who has encouraged me every step of the way to follow my dreams.

DeLinda Youngblood

We would like to express our appreciation to Pat Cunningham and Dottie Hall for all of their support and continual guidance as this book has grown from an idea to reality. But most of all, we would like to thank them for the development of the Four-Blocks® framework which has touched the lives of so many children and teachers. Thank you for making a difference in our lives!

Eve Hayes and DeLinda Youngblood

Table of Contents

Introduction

Rounding Up the Rhymes is an engaging, multilevel activity (Cunningham and Hall, 1997; Cunningham, Hall, and Sigmon, 1999). It was developed by Drs. Patricia Cunningham and Dorothy Hall to be used in the Working with Words Block, one of the four approaches for teaching reading in the comprehensive Four-Blocks® Literacy Model. It is appropriate to use the Rounding Up the Rhymes activity when most children have achieved phonemic awareness and have developed the ability to hear rhymes. Rounding Up the Rhymes is a great way to show students how rhymes work and how this knowledge will help them when they read and write (Cunningham, Hall, and Sigmon, 1999).

Rounding Up the Rhymes is usually introduced in first grade and continued into second grade. Students in third grade and beyond who do not yet indicate facility with the concept of rhyme, identification of rhyming words, and using spelling patterns and word families to help decode and spell other words will also benefit from this activity.

Rounding Up the Rhymes is used to follow up the reading of a book, story, or poem containing a number of rhyming words. The first reading of the selection could be during the teacher read-aloud in Self-Selected Reading, during Guided Reading, or during content-area time. The first and sometimes second reading of any text should focus on meaning and enjoyment. If a book is read during content-area time, the selection chosen is probably informational and supports the concepts of the study unit (theme) that the class is currently exploring. Books used for the Rounding Up the Rhymes activity become favorites for many students in the class. Putting these books in the baskets used for Self-Selected Reading means that these loved books can be reread many times, not only for enjoyment, but for the practice of reading and hearing the rhyming words in them.

In this book, we hope to provide support to teachers who enjoy using the Rounding Up the Rhymes activity to move their students forward in phonemic awareness, rhyming, and their understanding that rhymes can assist them as readers and writers. We have chosen to include books that have been popular with our own students. We have also included books that support curricular areas. Since seasons and holidays are some of our favorite times to use the Rounding Up the Rhymes activity, we have included several books to support these celebratory times in the classroom.

It is our hope that this book will help with the selection of books and lesson planning for teachers who want to use Rounding Up the Rhymes as a regular part of their language arts curriculum. We have included a list of the word families/spelling patterns matched to the books in which they can be found. There is a list of words to use in the transfer step of the activity. In the transfer step, students are encouraged to use the word knowledge they gain during a Rounding Up the Rhymes lesson in order to decode unknown words they encounter when reading and spell (encode) words when they are writing. Also provided is a support page for curriculum standards. Once it is filled out, teachers can see at a glance which word families/spelling patterns should be taught at their grade levels. This tool will be helpful as a cross reference of books to use to meet curriculum demands. There is also space to indicate the date(s) each word family/spelling pattern was introduced, reviewed, or formally assessed.

Even though there are many Working with Words Block activities, Rounding Up the Rhymes is one of our favorites. This is because the strategy is based on an authentic piece of literature, and children's literature is a passion we both share.

The Four-Blocks® Framework

The Four-Blocks® Literacy Model is a comprehensive approach for teaching language arts that was developed by Drs. Patricia Cunningham and Dorothy Hall in North Carolina during the late 1980s. It began in one first-grade classroom (Cunningham, Hall and Sigmon, 1999). This approach is now being used in first-, second-, and third-grade classrooms all over the world where teachers want to maximize their instructional time and meet the needs of students who are very diverse in their instructional needs and learning preferences.

The Four-Blocks® framework is a multi-method, multilevel approach that consists of Working with Words, Guided Reading, Self-Selected Reading, and Writing. The four blocks are incorporated every day and are critical in order to meet the different learning preferences of students. Incorporating each of the blocks every day honors the belief that children don't all learn the same way.

In order to meet the needs of children who are at different places in their literacy development, each of the four blocks needs to be as multilevel as possible. Strategies that provide support for struggling students and strategies that challenge students who are more proficient are used within each block. This multilevel approach ensures that all students—struggling, average, and excelling—are provided the support they need to continue to grow in their literacy development.

Each block requires about 30 to 40 minutes each day. Because each block receives equal time, children get sufficient support to continue to grow regardless of their learning preferences. Instruction in all four blocks can be delivered in two to two-and-a-half hours each day. (For more information about the Four-Blocks® Literacy Model, see *The Teacher's Guide to Four-Blocks®* by Cunningham, Hall and Sigmon. Or, visit *www.four-blocks.com*.)

Lesson Format

Step 1: Read the Book and Mark the Pages Containing Rhymes

Select a rhyming book with the rhyming patterns/word families that your students need to learn. Read the selected book to the children at least once for enjoyment and understanding before the Rounding Up the Rhymes lesson. You can read rhyming books to your students during the teacher read-aloud in Self-Selected Reading, during Guided Reading, or during content-area time. The initial reading of the book can be done on the same day as the lesson or on a previous day.

Prior to the Rounding Up the Rhymes lesson, use self-stick notes to mark the book pages containing the rhyming words you will focus on in the lesson. Include both rhyming words that are spelled alike and those that are spelled differently. You do not have to round up all of the rhymes. For the first few lessons (and maybe more if you have students who lack phonemic awareness), 8–10 rhymes is enough to "round up." The number of pages you mark will likely increase as students develop greater understanding and facility with this activity. Be sure to mark more pages with rhymes that have the same spelling pattern so that children will make the connection between the rhyming words and the spelling pattern. These are the rhymes that you will use in the transfer/extension segment of the lesson. As students begin to develop more understanding about how to use rhymes to help them read and write other words, you can increase the number of patterns extended and words transferred in any one lesson.

Step 2: Reread the Book and Round Up the Rhymes

During the Working with Words Block, take out the book again and reread the tagged pages, focusing on the rhyming words. As you read the pages with the rhyming words, encourage children to join in the reading and to listen for the rhymes they read. Children with limited phonemic awareness will be much more successful hearing rhymes when they have read aloud the words themselves rather than just listening for rhymes that you read aloud.

To provide concrete examples, Giles Andreae's wonderful book, *Rumble in the Jungle* (Tiger Tales, 2001) will be used throughout this explanation of Rounding Up the Rhymes.

When children identify the rhyming words as you reread the marked pages, write the words on index cards or sentence strips and place them in a pocket chart.

For example, as a teacher is rereading *Rumble in the Jungle*, students tell her that **paws** and **jaws** rhyme. The teacher writes those words on index cards and places them in the pocket chart. She repeats this procedure with **prey** and **way**.

Some of the rhyming words will have the same spelling pattern (**paws** and **jaws**) and others will not (**prey** and **way**). Continue with the reading until children have rounded up the rhymes from all of the marked pages.

Depending on the literacy levels of children in your classroom, some of them may not distinguish the difference between rhyming words and words that begin with the same sounds. You want these students to continue to participate, so try to respond to their contributions in a way that helps them learn to make this critical distinction.

The teacher who is using *Rumble in the Jungle* for her lesson might give supportive responses like this:

"I like your listening and thinking. Let's all say **horse**, **hippo**, **hurry**, and **hot**. All of these words sound alike at the beginning." She says them slowly, stretching out the words and emphasizing the beginning sounds.

"Do you hear the **h** at the beginning? **Horse**, **hippo**, **hurry**, and **hot** all begin with the same sound, but they don't rhyme.

"Now, let's add some words. Listen for the rhyming words when we say them—**horse**, **hippo**, **hurry**, **hot**, **hamster**, **hero**, **house**, **lot**. **Hot** and **lot** are the rhyming words. I'm going to write **hot** and **lot** on these cards (sentence strips, index cards, chart paper, transparencies, board) and put them in the pocket chart."

Continue having children participate and round up the rhymes with you until they have identified 8–10 sets of rhyming words, written them on index cards, and placed them in the pocket chart.

Some teachers prefer to use chart paper and a marker to write the words as children supply the rhymes. Other teachers enjoy using an overhead projector, transparencies, and erasable markers. One limitation of using an overhead projector is that the patterns and transfer words can't be posted in the classroom as a reminder and reference for the children to use. With a pocket chart or chart paper, the lesson can be posted in the classroom as student support for as long as the teacher feels it is beneficial. Some teachers prefer to have the word cards pre-written so that they can save time during the actual lesson.

Here is what the pocket chart would look like with rhymes that a class rounded up from *Rumble in the Jungle*.

paws	quivers	prey	hot
jaws	shivers	way	lot

hairy	best	polite	near	lights
scary	chest	night	fear	nights

There are many books with a large number of rhyming words. If there are too many sets of words for a lesson, just choose 8–10 pairs. You may want to choose other rhymes from the same book for subsequent Rounding Up the Rhymes lessons. Another reason to limit the number of rhyming words is time. Each lesson should last approximately 15–20 minutes. Otherwise, the lesson may become confusing or frustrating for some children.

Step 3: Observe Spelling Patterns and Identify Rhymes to Keep/Discard

Remind children that words which rhyme usually have the same spelling pattern, but not always. Review the idea that the spelling pattern in a short word begins with the first vowel and goes to the end of the word. For some students/classes, you may need to review which letters of the alphabet are the vowels.

Have students consider each set of rhyming words and identify the spelling pattern. They can come to the pocket chart or chart paper, underline the spelling pattern, and decide if the words are spelled the same. If you are using a pocket chart, the students can underline the pattern on the plastic strip using a dry erase marker. These marks can be easily wiped off after the lesson. Emphasize that in words with the same spelling pattern, the words sound alike and look alike. They can hear the rhyme and see the spelling pattern. Repeat this process for each set of rhyming words.

When you get to a set of words that rhyme but have different spelling patterns, remind students that rhyming words usually have the same spelling pattern, but not always. Explain to them that for the next part of this lesson, you only want to keep the words that sound alike and look alike—words that rhyme and have the same spelling pattern. Remove the word cards that do not have the same pattern, tear them up, and throw them in the trash can. This has a very dramatic impact on some children and helps to emphasize the importance of identifying those words that sound alike and are spelled the same. If you simply can't bring yourself to "trash" those word cards, consider having a special teacher's trash can so that those cards can be retrieved at a later time. You could also just set these cards to the side.

Continue with this process until all of the rhyming word sets have been considered. Keep those word sets that are spelled with the same pattern and discard those that are not spelled the same. You will now have several sets of words that rhyme and have the same spelling pattern in the pocket chart (or written on chart paper). Here is what the pocket chart would look like at this stage using the book *Rumble in the Jungle*.

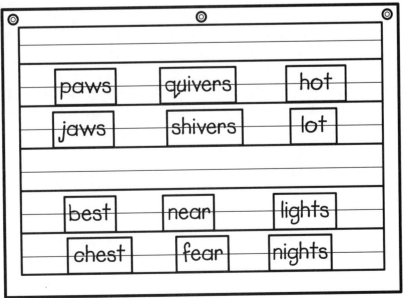

Step 4: Use Spelling Patterns for Transfer

The final part of this activity is the transfer step—using these rhyming words to read and write other words. This step is critical to the success of this activity for students whose thinking and learning does not go beyond what you explicitly teach. So far, you have taught students what rhyming words are. You have also taught them that some rhyming words are spelled alike, while others are not. Until you include this essential transfer step, the students have not learned anything they can actually use. The transfer step shows students how to use what they have learned to decode and spell other words.

Remind children that thinking of rhyming words they know can help them figure out unknown words when they are reading their books and stories. On an index card, write a word that rhymes with one of the rounded-up sets of words. Show it to students and have one of them put the new word with the rhyming set that has the same pattern. This will help students figure out how to decode the new word. Have students read the rounded-up words and then the new word, using the rhyme to help decode the new word. Here is an example using a set of rhyming words from *Rumble in the Jungle*.

"When you are reading books and stories, sometimes you come to new words that you don't know. You have to figure out these new words. One way to do that is to think about some rhyming words you already know that might help you to figure out the new word. If you were reading and came to this word (teacher shows **plot**), which words in the pocket chart would help you read this new word? That's right, **hot** and **lot**! **Hot** and **lot** have the same spelling pattern and they rhyme. **H-ot** and **l-ot**. Our new word **pl-ot** has the same spelling pattern as **hot** and **lot**. Let's read all three words—**hot**, **lot**, and **plot**. The new word rhymes with **hot** and **lot** and is spelled the same. Our new school is being built on a **plot** of ground behind our old school."

To scaffold toward independence, follow through with other examples that allow individual students to respond during this transfer step. Discreetly write a transfer word (in the *Rumble in the Jungle* example, **slot**) on a card and give it to a student. Ask the student to come to the chart and place the word with the other words that have the same spelling pattern. If the student's placement is correct, ask the class, "Is he right?" The class should respond that he is. Then, choose a student to explain why the word is in the right place. (For the *Rumble in the Jungle* example, the student should indicate that the word is in the right place because it has the same spelling pattern as **hot** and **lot**.) If the student's placement is incorrect, ask the class to take a look at a list of words while you spell each of them. (For the *Rumble in the Jungle* example, the teacher uses **near**, **fear**, and **slot**.) Now, ask the class if there is a better place for the word. Guide the student to find the spelling pattern that matches the word. (In the Rumble in the Jungle example, it is the **–ot** pattern).

Next, you want children to understand that they can also use their knowledge of rhyming patterns to help them spell words that they know how to say but do not yet know how to write correctly.

Here is an example using a set of rhyming words from *Rumble in the Jungle*. "Pretend you are writing and you need to write the word **claws**, as in the following sentence. 'The **claws** of the lion are sharp.' Which words in the pocket chart would help you know how to spell the word **claws** correctly? Exactly, **jaws** and **paws** can help you write the word **claws**. C-l and then the same spelling pattern **a-w-s** as in **jaws** and **paws**. You have the word **claws**."

Continue this with several more words—some to read and some to write. Here is an example of what the pocket chart for *Rumble in the Jungle* might look like with the spelling patterns that have been extended to new words to read and write. Some of the transfer words need to be easy and some need to be more challenging.

paws	quivers	hot	best	near	lights
jaws	shivers	lot	chest	fear	nights
claws	rivers	plot	test	ear	fights
straws	slivers	slot	crest	gear	flights
outlaws	delivers	teapot	invest	shear	knights

Step 5: Mad Minute (optional)

Select one of the patterns from the lesson and write it on the board. Choose a student to go to the board and write as many words as she can think of that are spelled with that pattern. Give the student one minute. The words must be real words, not nonsense words. Encourage the student to use the alphabet chart to help her think of words. (Adding blends and digraphs over each letter of the alphabet chart can provide further assistance for students.) While the student is writing, the rest of the class is also generating a list of words spelled with the pattern. This list could be a mental one or on paper. At the end of the minute, ask the class to read the words on the board together. If students aren't sure if a word is a real one, ask the Mad Minute student to use the word in a sentence to see if it makes sense. After the words have been read, ask the rest of the class to share any other new words that they thought of during the minute. The Mad Minute student adds these words to the list on the board as other students share. Check with a rhyming dictionary to see if there are additional words that the students didn't identify. Be prepared for transfer excitement during this activity!

One of the major components of the Four-Blocks® Literacy Model is that each of the four blocks is as multilevel as possible. The criteria that make an activity multilevel are:

- There are multiple things to be learned.

- The teacher interacts with students based on each child's instructional needs.

- All students experience success.

(Cunningham, Moore, Cunningham, and Moore, 2004).

In a Rounding Up the Rhymes lesson, students who are in the initial stages of phonemic awareness, often our most struggling students, learn what rhymes are. They also learn how to distinguish rhyming words from words with the same beginning sounds. Students who are further along in their phonemic awareness learn that rhyming words often share the same spelling patterns. In addition, they learn a great deal about spelling patterns. Students who are the most advanced learn how to use these spelling patterns when reading unknown words and writing words they know. This advanced decoding and spelling ability becomes evident in the increased reading fluency and more fully developed phonetic spellings of students who are at higher proficiency levels (Cunningham, 1997). The transfer step in the Rounding Up the Rhymes lesson also provides wonderful opportunities to enhance students' vocabularies by asking them to read words that may be new to them or that are less commonly encountered.

If you make each lesson multilevel, all students will experience success and will move forward in their understanding of how to use what they know about rhymes when they really need to—when they decode in their reading and when they spell in their writing.

Rounding Up the Rhymes

Sample Lesson Plan
Grade 1
Somewhere in the Ocean by Jennifer Ward and T. J. Marsh
(Rising Moon Books, 2000)

1. Read the book for students' enjoyment and understanding. (Self-Selected Reading, Guided Reading, or content area)
2. Decide how much of the text you will use for this activity (entire book or specific pages). If you are only revisiting specific pages, mark the pages to be used.
3. During Working with Words, reread the pages you've marked, having students listen for and identify the rhyming words.
4. As you are reading, write the rhyming words that children identify on index cards and display them in a pocket chart (or write the words on a piece of chart paper).
5. Have students consider each set of rhyming words. Keep rhyming words with the same spelling patterns. Discard rhyming words that are not spelled alike.

Rhymes to keep			Rhymes to discard	
thrive	five		run	one
mix	six		blue	two
line	nine		anemone	three
den	ten		shore	four

6. Transfer/extend the spelling patterns of the rhyming words you keep to new words to read and write.

Words to extend/transfer for each spelling pattern

dive	hive	drive	
fix	nix	affix	
dine	fine	swine	tine
hen	men	wren	

Rounding Up the Rhymes

Sample Lesson Plan
Grade 1

Wild About Books by Judy Sierra
(Knopf Books for Young Readers, 2004)

1. Read the book for students' enjoyment and understanding. (Self-Selected Reading, Guided Reading, or content area)
2. Decide how much of the text you will use for this activity (entire book or specific pages). If you are only revisiting specific pages, mark the pages to be used.
3. During Working with Words, reread the pages you've marked, having students listen for and identify the rhyming words.
4. As you are reading, write the rhyming words that children identify on index cards and display them in a pocket chart (or write the words on a piece of chart paper).
5. Have students consider each set of rhyming words. Keep rhyming words with the same spelling patterns. Discard rhyming words that are not spelled alike.

Rhymes to keep			Rhymes to discard	
fat	hat	cat	Seuss	moose
bill(s)	quill(s)		new	too

6. Transfer/extend the spelling patterns of the rhyming words you keep to new words to read and write.

Words to extend/transfer for each spelling pattern

bat	sat	mat	vat	chat	splat
hill	mill	skill	trill	refill	

Rounding Up the Rhymes

Sample Lesson Plan
Grade 2

More Parts by Tedd Arnold
(Puffin Books, 2003)

1. Read the book for students' enjoyment and understanding. (Self-Selected Reading, Guided Reading, or content area)
2. Decide how much of the text you will use for this activity (entire book or specific pages). If you are only revisiting specific pages, mark the pages to be used.
3. During Working with Words, reread the pages you've marked, having students listen for and identify the rhyming words.
4. As you are reading, write the rhyming words that children identify on index cards and display them in a pocket chart (or write the words on a piece of chart paper).
5. Have students consider each set of rhyming words. Keep rhyming words with the same spelling patterns. Discard rhyming words that are not spelled alike.

Rhymes to keep		Rhymes to discard	
understand	hand	new	do
hear	fear	apart	heart
room	doom	lie	try
okay	say		

6. Transfer/extend the spelling patterns of the rhyming words you keep to new words to read and write.

Words to extend/transfer for each spelling pattern

band	gland	strand	cowhand	demand
dear	gear	shear	clear	spear
boom	loom	broom	gloom	zoom
bay	gray	play	spray	sway

Rounding Up the Rhymes

Sample Lesson Plan
Grade 2

Wild About Books by Judy Sierra
(Knopf Books for Young Readers, 2004)

1. Read the book for students' enjoyment and understanding. (Self-Selected Reading, Guided Reading, or content area)
2. Decide how much of the text you will use for this activity (entire book or specific pages). If you are only revisiting specific pages, mark the pages to be used.
3. During Working with Words, reread the pages you've marked, having students listen for and identify the rhyming words.
4. As you are reading, write the rhyming words that children identify on index cards and display them in a pocket chart (or write the words on a piece of chart paper).
5. Have students consider each set of rhyming words. Keep rhyming words with the same spelling patterns. Discard rhyming words that are not spelled alike.

Rhymes to keep			Rhymes to discard		
stair	chair		lynx	skinks	
well	tell		new	true	how-to
nook(s)	book(s)		Chinese	please	
tall	small	mall			

6. Transfer/extend the spelling patterns of the rhyming words you keep to new words to read and write.

Words to extend/transfer for each spelling pattern

fair	flair	lair	midair	repair	
dwell	jell	swell	farewell	retell	unwell
cook	look	brook	shook	unhook	
call	stall	install			

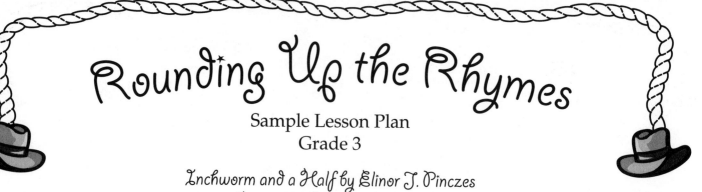

Rounding Up the Rhymes

Sample Lesson Plan
Grade 3

Inchworm and a Half by Elinor J. Pinczes
(Houghton Mifflin, 2003)

1. Read the book for students' enjoyment and understanding. (Self-Selected Reading, Guided Reading, or content area)
2. Decide how much of the text you will use for this activity (entire book or specific pages). If you are only revisiting specific pages, mark the pages to be used.
3. During Working with Words, reread the pages you've marked, having students listen for and identify the rhyming words.
4. As you are reading, write the rhyming words that children identify on index cards and display them in a pocket chart (or write the words on a piece of chart paper).
5. Have students consider each set of rhyming words. Keep rhyming words with the same spelling patterns. Discard rhyming words that are not spelled alike.

Rhymes to keep		Rhymes to discard	
end	depend	ease	peas
hoop	loop	three	be
wrong	along	air	there
twice	nice		

6. Transfer/extend the spelling patterns of the rhyming words you keep to new words to read and write.

Words to extend/transfer for each spelling pattern

bend	fend	blend	spend	trend
coop	droop	troop	whoop	
tong	prong	strong		
dice	price	splice	device	

Rounding Up the Rhymes

Sample Lesson Plan
Grade 3

Wild About Books by Judy Sierra
(Knopf Books for Young Readers, 2004)

1. Read the book for students' enjoyment and understanding. (Self-Selected Reading, Guided Reading, or content area)
2. Decide how much of the text you will use for this activity (entire book or specific pages). If you are only revisiting specific pages, mark the pages to be used.
3. During Working with Words, reread the pages you've marked, having students listen for and identify the rhyming words.
4. As you are reading, write the rhyming words that children identify on index cards and display them in a pocket chart (or write the words on a piece of chart paper).
5. Have students consider each set of rhyming words. Keep rhyming words with the same spelling patterns. Discard rhyming words that are not spelled alike.

Rhymes to keep		Rhymes to discard		
bunch(es)	lunch(es)	stampede(ing)	read(ing)	
right	tight	snake(s)	ache(s)	
shape	ape	zoo	haiku	review
mind	find	surprise	prize	

6. Transfer/extend the spelling patterns of the rhyming words you keep to new words to read and write.

Words to extend/transfer for each spelling pattern

munch	punch	brunch	crunch	scrunch
fight	light	blight	plight	knight
cape	gape	drape	reshape	escape
bind	rind	grind	blind	unwind

The 10 Best Things About My Dad

by Christine Loomis (Scholastic Paperbacks, 2004)

ISBN 0-43957-769-1

Summary: A boy shares the 10 best things that he loves about his dad.

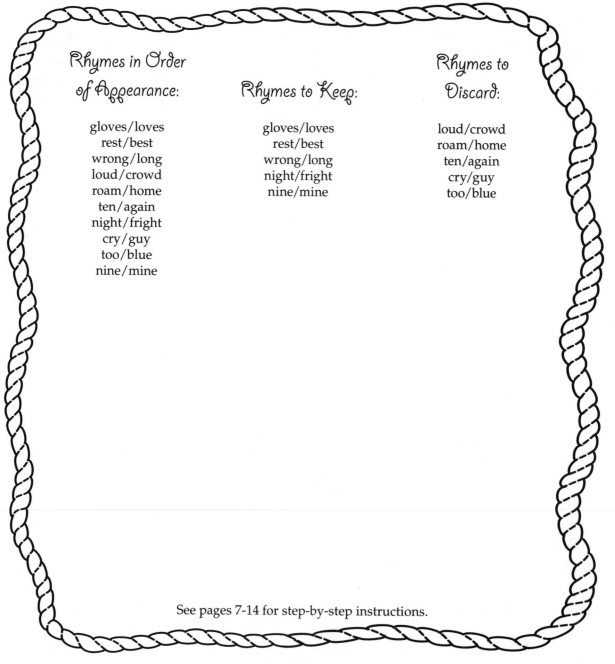

Rhymes in Order of Appearance:	Rhymes to Keep:	Rhymes to Discard:
gloves/loves	gloves/loves	loud/crowd
rest/best	rest/best	roam/home
wrong/long	wrong/long	ten/again
loud/crowd	night/fright	cry/guy
roam/home	nine/mine	too/blue
ten/again		
night/fright		
cry/guy		
too/blue		
nine/mine		

See pages 7-14 for step-by-step instructions.

Angel Pig and the Hidden Christmas

by Jan L. Waldron (Puffin Books, 2000)

ISBN 0-14056-591-4

Summary: When the pigs realize they don't have money for Christmas gifts, they begin an adventure of finding the true meaning of this special season.

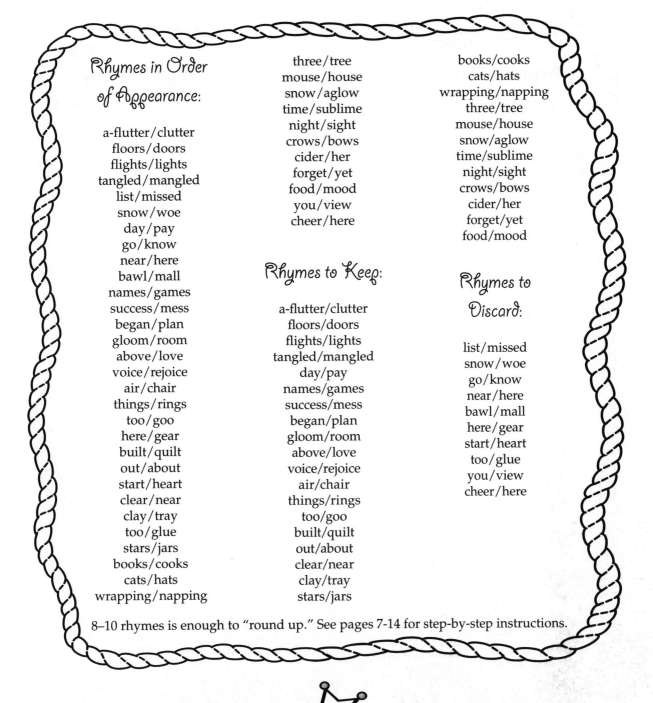

Rhymes in Order of Appearance:

a-flutter/clutter
floors/doors
flights/lights
tangled/mangled
list/missed
snow/woe
day/pay
go/know
near/here
bawl/mall
names/games
success/mess
began/plan
gloom/room
above/love
voice/rejoice
air/chair
things/rings
too/goo
here/gear
built/quilt
out/about
start/heart
clear/near
clay/tray
too/glue
stars/jars
books/cooks
cats/hats
wrapping/napping

three/tree
mouse/house
snow/aglow
time/sublime
night/sight
crows/bows
cider/her
forget/yet
food/mood
you/view
cheer/here

Rhymes to Keep:

a-flutter/clutter
floors/doors
flights/lights
tangled/mangled
day/pay
names/games
success/mess
began/plan
gloom/room
above/love
voice/rejoice
air/chair
things/rings
too/goo
built/quilt
out/about
clear/near
clay/tray
stars/jars

books/cooks
cats/hats
wrapping/napping
three/tree
mouse/house
snow/aglow
time/sublime
night/sight
crows/bows
cider/her
forget/yet
food/mood

Rhymes to Discard:

list/missed
snow/woe
go/know
near/here
bawl/mall
here/gear
start/heart
too/glue
you/view
cheer/here

8–10 rhymes is enough to "round up." See pages 7-14 for step-by-step instructions.

The Bear Came Over to My House

by Rick Walton (Puffin Books, 2003)

ISBN 0-69811-988-6

Summary: Follow the antics of the bear as he comes over for a visit. He moves from one perilous situation to another. This text offers the opportunity to emphasize prediction, verb tenses, and question/response.

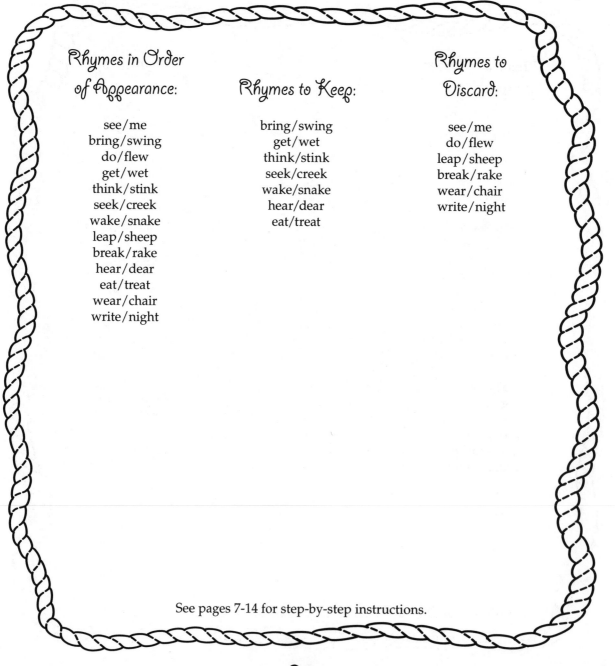

Rhymes in Order of Appearance:

see/me
bring/swing
do/flew
get/wet
think/stink
seek/creek
wake/snake
leap/sheep
break/rake
hear/dear
eat/treat
wear/chair
write/night

Rhymes to Keep:

bring/swing
get/wet
think/stink
seek/creek
wake/snake
hear/dear
eat/treat

Rhymes to Discard:

see/me
do/flew
leap/sheep
break/rake
wear/chair
write/night

See pages 7-14 for step-by-step instructions.

Bear Wants More

by Karma Wilson (Margaret K. McElderry Books, 2003)

ISBN 0-68984-509-X

Summary: Bear wakes up and is ravenous. He and his friends proceed to find enough food to satisfy the bear's appetite.

Rhymes in Order of Appearance:

den/thin
around/ground
lawn/gone
pail/Vale
back/snack
sweet/eat
Hare/Bear
me/tree
lunch/crunch
pole/hole
shore/more
den/wren
lair/Bear
tummy/yummy
blows/nose
den/in
luck/stuck
tight/might
hard/yard
wide/outside
cakes/aches
snores/more

Rhymes to Keep:

around/ground
back/snack
lunch/crunch
pole/hole
shore/more
den/wren
tummy/yummy
luck/stuck
tight/might
hard/yard
wide/outside

Rhymes to Discard:

den/thin
lawn/gone
pail/Vale
sweet/eat
Hare/Bear
me/tree
lair/Bear
blows/nose
den/in
cakes/aches
snores/more

8–10 rhymes is enough to "round up." See pages 7-14 for step-by-step instructions.

Rounding Up the Rhymes • Grades 1–3

Belly Button Boy

by Peter Maloney and Felicia Zekauskas (Puffin Books, 2003)

ISBN 0-14250-017-8

Summary: Billy is a little boy who enjoys getting dirty and is not the least bit concerned that dirt is piling up in his belly button. When a seed begins to sprout, his troubles begin.

Rhymes in Order of Appearance:	Rhymes to Keep:	Rhymes to Discard:
better/sweater	sand/hand	better/sweater
sand/hand	cup/up	dirt/hurt
dirt/hurt	grout/sprout	morning/warning
cup/up	stood/good	jeer/hear
grout/sprout	share/stare	sleeves/leaves
morning/warning	himself/bookshelf	him/limb
stood/good	grow/know	nurse/worse
share/stare	stall/tall	pallid/salad
jeer/hear	room/bloom	her/doctor
sleeves/leaves	reveal/conceal	flus/news
himself/bookshelf	need/weed	physician/condition
grow/know	say/day	eyes/surprise
him/limb		fruited/uprooted
stall/tall		it/it
nurse/worse		pardon/garden
room/bloom		green/clean
reveal/conceal		toe/go
need/weed		
pallid/salad		
her/doctor		
flus/news		
physician/condition		
say/day		
eyes/surprise		
fruited/uprooted		
it/it		
pardon/garden		
green/clean		
toe/go		

8–10 rhymes is enough to "round up." See pages 7-14 for step-by-step instructions.

The Best Vacation Ever

by Stuart J. Murphy (HarperTrophy, 1997)

ISBN 0-06446-706-6

Summary: The main character helps her family decide where to go on vacation by collecting data to find the perfect spot.

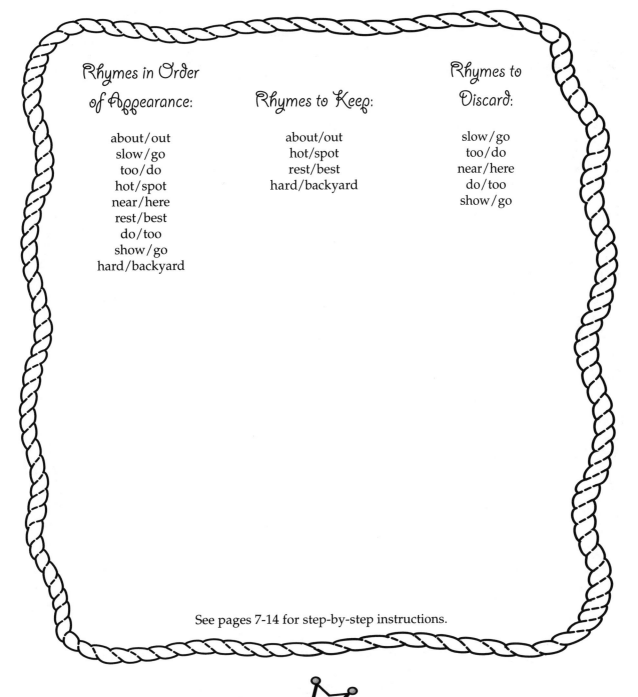

Rhymes in Order of Appearance:

about/out
slow/go
too/do
hot/spot
near/here
rest/best
do/too
show/go
hard/backyard

Rhymes to Keep:

about/out
hot/spot
rest/best
hard/backyard

Rhymes to Discard:

slow/go
too/do
near/here
do/too
show/go

See pages 7-14 for step-by-step instructions.

27

Birds Build Nests

by Yvonne Winer (Charlesbridge Publishing, 2002)

ISBN 1-57091-501-6

Summary: This book shows the diversity of interesting nesting techniques that birds use to protect their eggs and young. Beautiful illustrations accompany the text. The text contains many words that provide opportunities for vocabulary enhancement. In addition to the rhyming text, there is a nest identification guide at the end of the book.

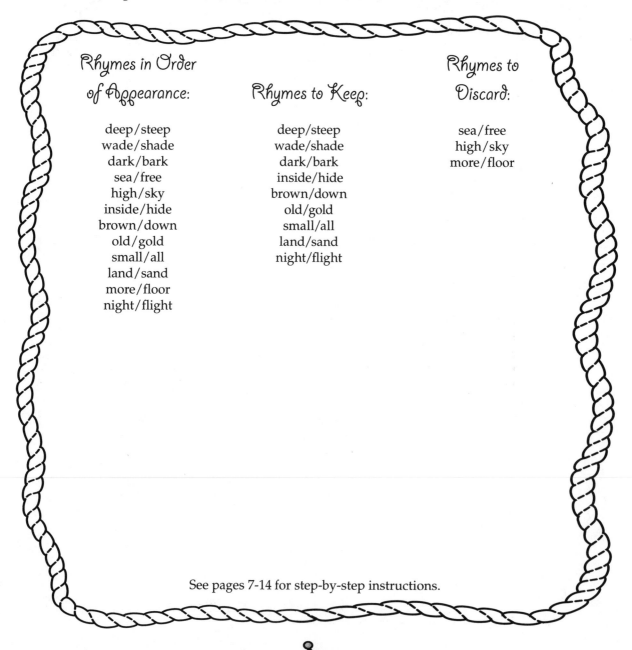

Rhymes in Order of Appearance:	Rhymes to Keep:	Rhymes to Discard:
deep/steep	deep/steep	sea/free
wade/shade	wade/shade	high/sky
dark/bark	dark/bark	more/floor
sea/free	inside/hide	
high/sky	brown/down	
inside/hide	old/gold	
brown/down	small/all	
old/gold	land/sand	
small/all	night/flight	
land/sand		
more/floor		
night/flight		

See pages 7-14 for step-by-step instructions.

The Brand New Kid

by Katie Couric (Doubleday, 2000)

ISBN 0-38550-030-0

Summary: Lazlo S. Gasky goes to a new school and finds that being the brand new kid is not so great. He eventually finds a friend in a girl named Ellie and together they show the other students the importance of acceptance.

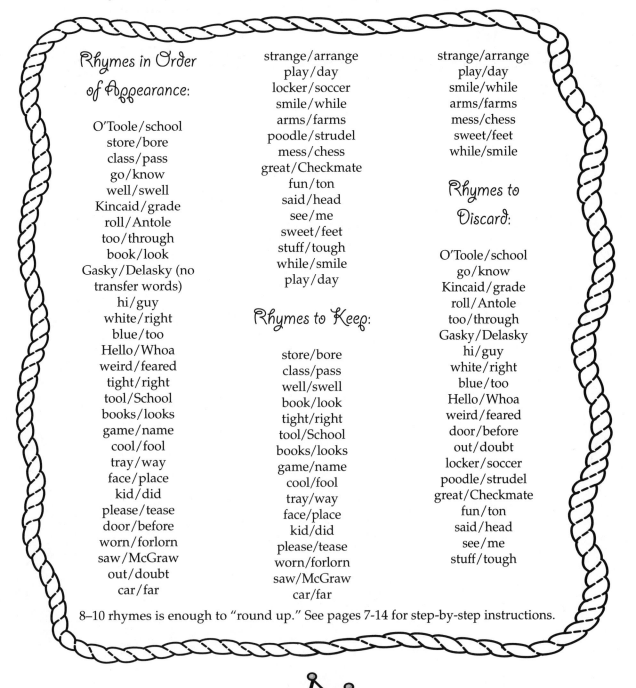

Rhymes in Order of Appearance:

O'Toole/school
store/bore
class/pass
go/know
well/swell
Kincaid/grade
roll/Antole
too/through
book/look
Gasky/Delasky (no transfer words)
hi/guy
white/right
blue/too
Hello/Whoa
weird/feared
tight/right
tool/School
books/looks
game/name
cool/fool
tray/way
face/place
kid/did
please/tease
door/before
worn/forlorn
saw/McGraw
out/doubt
car/far

strange/arrange
play/day
locker/soccer
smile/while
arms/farms
poodle/strudel
mess/chess
great/Checkmate
fun/ton
said/head
see/me
sweet/feet
stuff/tough
while/smile
play/day

Rhymes to Keep:

store/bore
class/pass
well/swell
book/look
tight/right
tool/School
books/looks
game/name
cool/fool
tray/way
face/place
kid/did
please/tease
worn/forlorn
saw/McGraw
car/far

strange/arrange
play/day
smile/while
arms/farms
mess/chess
sweet/feet
while/smile

Rhymes to Discard:

O'Toole/school
go/know
Kincaid/grade
roll/Antole
too/through
Gasky/Delasky
hi/guy
white/right
blue/too
Hello/Whoa
weird/feared
door/before
out/doubt
locker/soccer
poodle/strudel
great/Checkmate
fun/ton
said/head
see/me
stuff/tough

8–10 rhymes is enough to "round up." See pages 7-14 for step-by-step instructions.

Butterflies Fly

by Yvonne Winer (Charlesbridge Publishing, 2001)

ISBN 1-57091-447-8

Summary: This rhyming book shares information about different habitats of butterflies with a butterfly guide in the back.

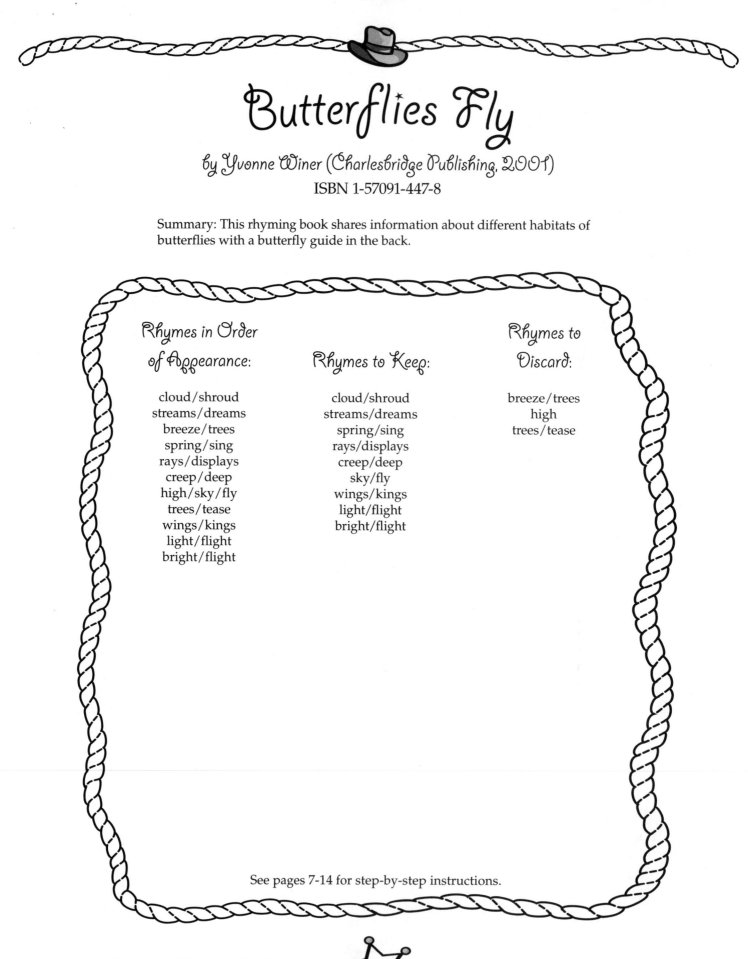

Rhymes in Order of Appearance:

cloud/shroud
streams/dreams
breeze/trees
spring/sing
rays/displays
creep/deep
high/sky/fly
trees/tease
wings/kings
light/flight
bright/flight

Rhymes to Keep:

cloud/shroud
streams/dreams
spring/sing
rays/displays
creep/deep
sky/fly
wings/kings
light/flight
bright/flight

Rhymes to Discard:

breeze/trees
high
trees/tease

See pages 7-14 for step-by-step instructions.

Counting Is for the Birds

by Frank Mazzola, Jr. (Charlesbridge Publishing, 1997)

ISBN 0-88106-950-7

Summary: Number concepts are emphasized as students enjoy this text about birds at a feeder. Also included is information about the kinds of birds featured in the book.

Rhymes in Order of Appearance:

overhead/fed
around/found
wait/great
catch/snatch
feet/beat
view/two
mate/rate
beak/peek
wood/good
high/sky
fast/past
speed/lead
share/fare
ground/sound
stare/lair
arrive/thrive
fill/skill
too/blue
about/out
array/away
chance/glance
in/spin
size/surprise
here/fear
feast/beast
sight/mid-flight
here/near
fun/done
treat/street

Rhymes to Keep:

around/found
catch/snatch
mate/rate
wood/good
fast/past
share/fare
ground/sound
arrive/thrive
fill/skill
about/out
array/away
chance/glance
in/spin
feast/beast
sight/mid-flight

Rhymes to Discard:

overhead/fed
wait/great
feet/beat
view/two
beak/peek
high/sky
speed/lead
stare/lair
too/blue
size/surprise
here/fear
here/near
fun/done
treat/street

8–10 rhymes is enough to "round up." See pages 7-14 for step-by-step instructions.

The Crayon Box that Talked

by Shane DeRolf (Random House Books for Young Readers, 1997)

ISBN 0-67988-611-7

Summary: Spend a day with a little girl as she shows a box of crayons how to get along; by working together, their differences can create a beautiful picture.

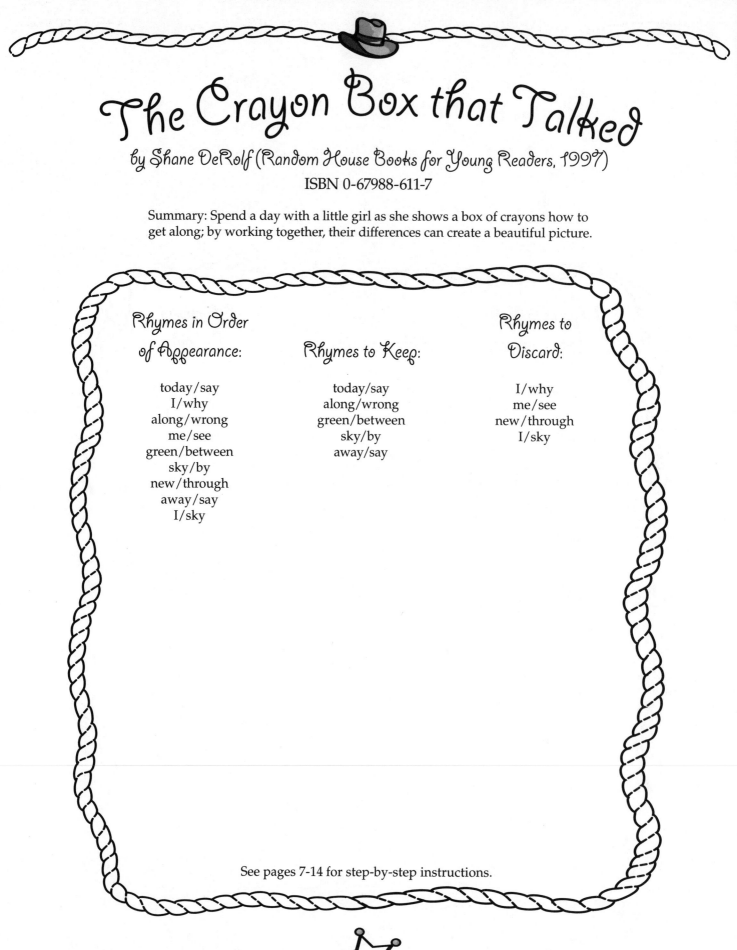

Rhymes in Order of Appearance:

today/say
I/why
along/wrong
me/see
green/between
sky/by
new/through
away/say
I/sky

Rhymes to Keep:

today/say
along/wrong
green/between
sky/by
away/say

Rhymes to Discard:

I/why
me/see
new/through
I/sky

See pages 7-14 for step-by-step instructions.

32

Don't Call Me Pig!

by Conrad J. Storad (RGU Group, 1999)

ISBN 1-89179-501-5

Summary: Told from the perspective of a Javelina on the Southwestern desert, this fun rhyming book is full of information about this Collared Peccary.

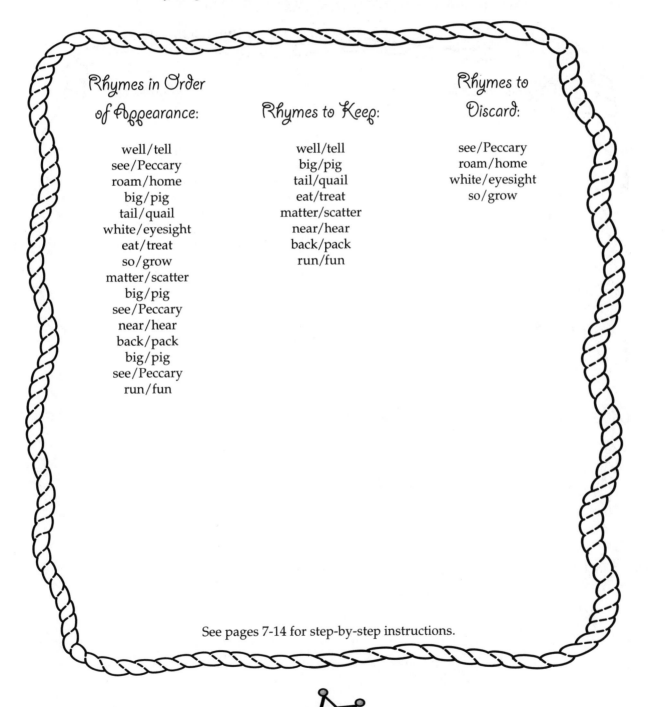

Rhymes in Order of Appearance:

well/tell
see/Peccary
roam/home
big/pig
tail/quail
white/eyesight
eat/treat
so/grow
matter/scatter
big/pig
see/Peccary
near/hear
back/pack
big/pig
see/Peccary
run/fun

Rhymes to Keep:

well/tell
big/pig
tail/quail
eat/treat
matter/scatter
near/hear
back/pack
run/fun

Rhymes to Discard:

see/Peccary
roam/home
white/eyesight
so/grow

See pages 7-14 for step-by-step instructions.

Each Peach Pear Plum

by Janet and Allan Ahlberg (Puffin Books, 1986)

ISBN 0-14050-639-X

Summary: This book provides a wonderful opportunity to emphasize "reading" the pictures to find the fairy tale characters that are hidden within each illustration.

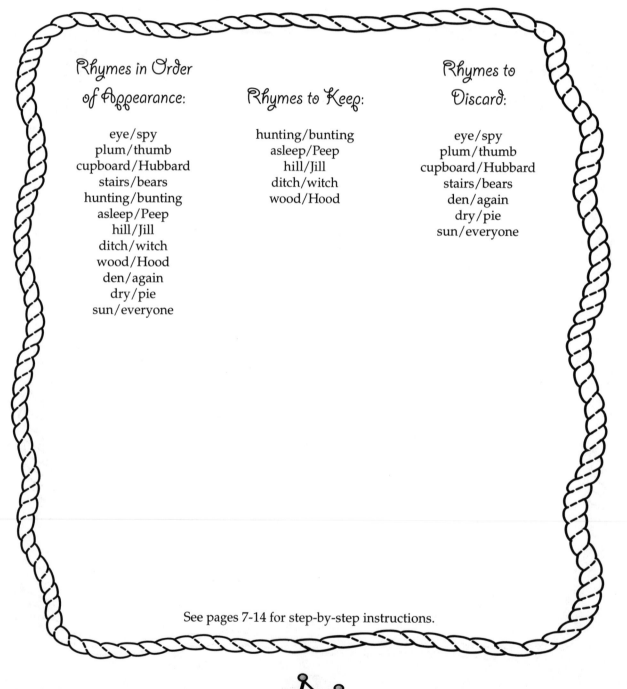

Rhymes in Order of Appearance:

eye/spy
plum/thumb
cupboard/Hubbard
stairs/bears
hunting/bunting
asleep/Peep
hill/Jill
ditch/witch
wood/Hood
den/again
dry/pie
sun/everyone

Rhymes to Keep:

hunting/bunting
asleep/Peep
hill/Jill
ditch/witch
wood/Hood

Rhymes to Discard:

eye/spy
plum/thumb
cupboard/Hubbard
stairs/bears
den/again
dry/pie
sun/everyone

See pages 7-14 for step-by-step instructions.

The Flea's Sneeze

by Lynn Downey (Henry Holt and Co., 2000)

ISBN 0-80506-103-7

Summary: Nobody on the farm notices, but the flea has a cold. His sneeze causes quite a commotion among the animals. Everything ends peacefully—almost.

Rhymes in Order of Appearance:

cat/bat
owl/fowl
hog/frog
mouse/house
plea/be
rat/cat/bat
blue/moo
nose/doze
frog/log/hog
wheeze/sneeze

Rhymes to Keep:

cat/bat
owl/fowl
hog/frog
mouse/house
rat/cat/bat
frog/log/hog
wheeze/sneeze

Rhymes to Discard:

plea/be
blue/moo
nose/doze

See pages 7-14 for step-by-step instructions.

Follow Me!

by Bethany Roberts (Clarion Books, 1998)

ISBN 0-39582-268-8

Summary: A mother octopus takes her new babies out on a tour of the ocean waters. They meet all kinds of creatures, including some that are very dangerous. The rhyming text introduces children to ocean biome vocabulary.

Rhymes in Order of Appearance:	Rhymes to Keep:	Rhymes to Discard:
row/go	play/way	row/go
play/way	weeds/reeds	see/me
see/me	fish/swish	homes/foam
weeds/reeds	seek/peek	soar/floor
fish/swish	sway/play	
homes/foam	ink/sink	
seek/peek	zip/ship	
sway/play	wall/all	
ink/sink		
soar/floor		
zip/ship		
wall/all		

See pages 7-14 for step-by-step instructions.

Get Up and Go!

by Stuart J. Murphy (HarperTrophy, 1996)
ISBN 0-06446-704-X

Summary: It is Sammie the dog's job to make sure the little girl gets up and makes it to the bus on time. Using a timeline, she makes it with no time to spare.

Rhymes in Order of Appearance:

slow/go
Teddy/ready
take/make
try/by
most/toast
treat/eat
do/too
hair/care
need/read
why/by
find/behind
door/more
late/great
ready/Teddy
one/done
fine/mine

Rhymes to Keep:

take/make
try/by
treat/eat
why/by
find/behind
one/done
fine/mine

Rhymes to Discard:

slow/go
Teddy/ready
most/toast
do/too
hair/care
need/read
door/more
late/great
ready/Teddy

8–10 rhymes is enough to "round up." See pages 7-14 for step-by-step instructions.

Giraffes Can't Dance

by Giles Andreae (Scholastic, 2001)

ISBN 0-43928-719-7

Summary: Gerald feels so ashamed because he can't dance like the other animals. As the jungle dance approaches, he is very worried. On that fateful night, he discovers his own uniqueness and begins to believe in himself.

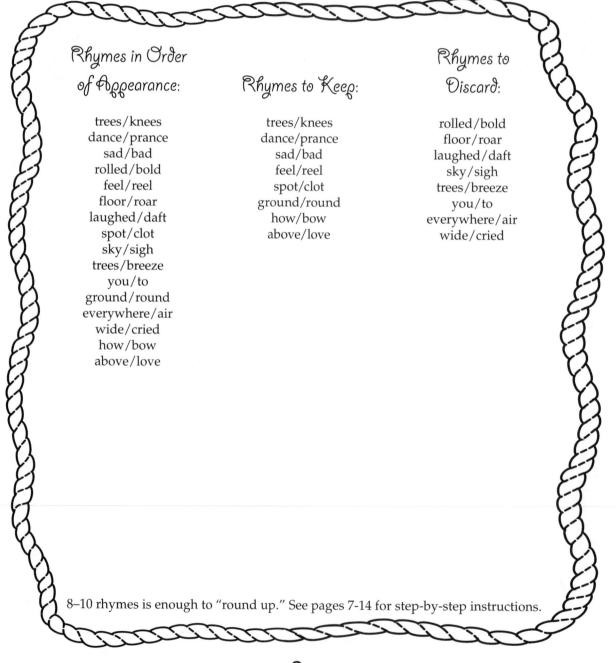

Rhymes in Order of Appearance:	Rhymes to Keep:	Rhymes to Discard:
trees/knees	trees/knees	rolled/bold
dance/prance	dance/prance	floor/roar
sad/bad	sad/bad	laughed/daft
rolled/bold	feel/reel	sky/sigh
feel/reel	spot/clot	trees/breeze
floor/roar	ground/round	you/to
laughed/daft	how/bow	everywhere/air
spot/clot	above/love	wide/cried
sky/sigh		
trees/breeze		
you/to		
ground/round		
everywhere/air		
wide/cried		
how/bow		
above/love		

8–10 rhymes is enough to "round up." See pages 7-14 for step-by-step instructions.

Goodnight Moon

by Margaret Wise Brown (HarperTrophy, 1977)
ISBN 0-06443-017-0

Summary: A little rabbit says, "Goodnight" to all of the familiar belongings in his great green room as nighttime slowly closes in and his room gradually becomes darker.

Rhymes in Order of Appearance:

balloon/moon
toyhouse/mouse
brush/mush/hush
bears/chairs
kittens/mittens
clocks/socks
house/mouse
air/everywhere

Rhymes to Keep:

balloon/moon
toyhouse/mouse
brush/mush/hush
kittens/mittens
clocks/socks
house/mouse

Rhymes to Discard:

bears/chairs
air/everywhere

See pages 7-14 for step-by-step instructions.

Green Wilma

by Tedd Arnold (Puffin Books, 1998)

ISBN 0-14056-362-8

Summary: When Wilma wakes up she surprisingly finds herself green and has a strong desire to eat flies. Excitement follows her throughout the school day. Prepare for an unexpected ending.

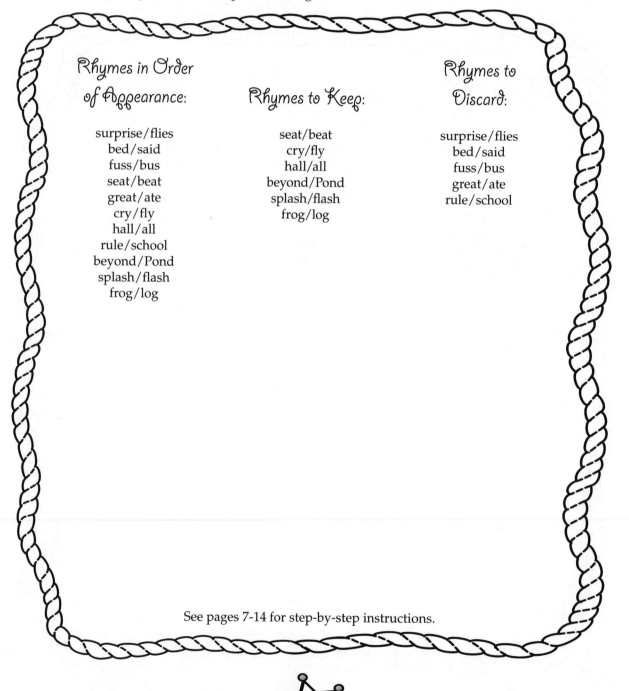

Rhymes in Order of Appearance:

surprise/flies
bed/said
fuss/bus
seat/beat
great/ate
cry/fly
hall/all
rule/school
beyond/Pond
splash/flash
frog/log

Rhymes to Keep:

seat/beat
cry/fly
hall/all
beyond/Pond
splash/flash
frog/log

Rhymes to Discard:

surprise/flies
bed/said
fuss/bus
great/ate
rule/school

See pages 7-14 for step-by-step instructions.

40

The Grumpy Morning

by Pamela Duncan Edwards (Hyperion, 1998)

ISBN 0-78680-331-2

Summary: The farm animals are awake and ready for breakfast but become upset when they discover that no one is there to feed them.

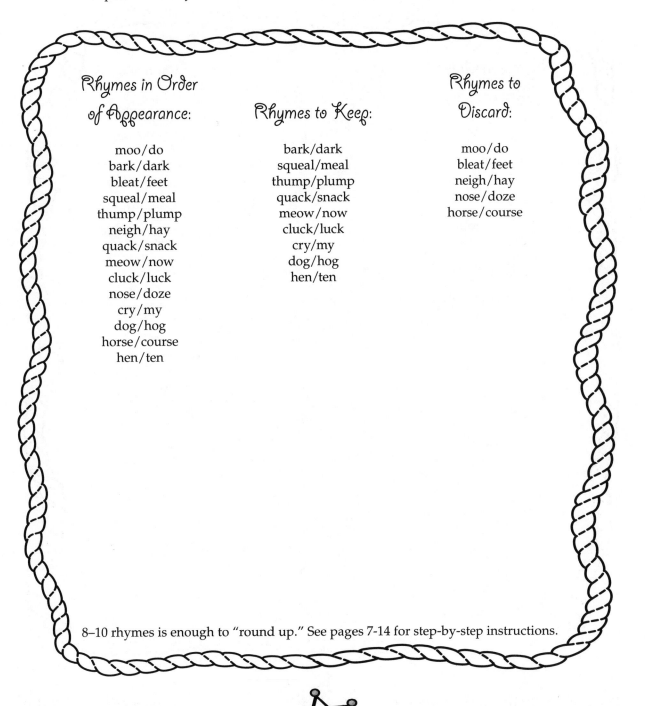

Rhymes in Order of Appearance:

moo/do
bark/dark
bleat/feet
squeal/meal
thump/plump
neigh/hay
quack/snack
meow/now
cluck/luck
nose/doze
cry/my
dog/hog
horse/course
hen/ten

Rhymes to Keep:

bark/dark
squeal/meal
thump/plump
quack/snack
meow/now
cluck/luck
cry/my
dog/hog
hen/ten

Rhymes to Discard:

moo/do
bleat/feet
neigh/hay
nose/doze
horse/course

8–10 rhymes is enough to "round up." See pages 7-14 for step-by-step instructions.

Hello School!

by Dee Lillegard (Dragonfly Books, 2003)

ISBN 0-44041-777-5

Summary: Familiar schoolroom objects are the subjects of these verses, which show hidden personalities one would never expect to encounter in a classroom.

Rhymes in Order of Appearance:

wait/late
walk/talk
filled/thrilled
large/charge
face/erase
about/out
head/instead
shut/cut
grin/thin
Z/free
birds/words
yum/tum
too/you
day/play/way
sky/fly
Go/slow
more/floor/snore
hide/wide
on/gone
sunny/runny/funny
birdie/sturdy
mess/yes
scene/green
hours/flowers
mind/behind
seat/feet
whether/together
mumble/fumble/jumble/
grumble/tumble
vroom/room/zoom

way/today
too/do
out/snout
feet/sheet
hue/new
rum/tum
bam/am
okay/play
shake/make
know/go
sigh/bye

Rhymes to Keep:

walk/talk
filled/thrilled
large/charge
about/out
head/instead
shut/cut
grin/thin
yum/tum
day/play/way
sky/fly
more/snore
hide/wide
sunny/funny/runny
mind/behind
whether/together
mumble/fumble/jumble/
grumble/tumble
vroom/room/zoom
way/today
out/snout

feet/sheet
rum/tum
bam/am
okay/play
shake/make

Rhymes to Discard:

wait/late
face/erase
Z/free
birds/words
too/you
Go/slow
floor
on/gone
birdie/sturdy
mess/yes
scene/green
hours/flowers
seat/feet
too/do
hue/new
know/go
sigh/bye

8–10 rhymes is enough to "round up." See pages 7-14 for step-by-step instructions.

Hooray for You!

by Marianne Richmond (Marianne Richmond Studios, Inc., 2001)

ISBN 0-93167-444-1

Summary: There is no other human being just like you. We all need to celebrate our uniqueness. Take a head-to-toe journey and explore with delight the individualism that makes each one of us special.

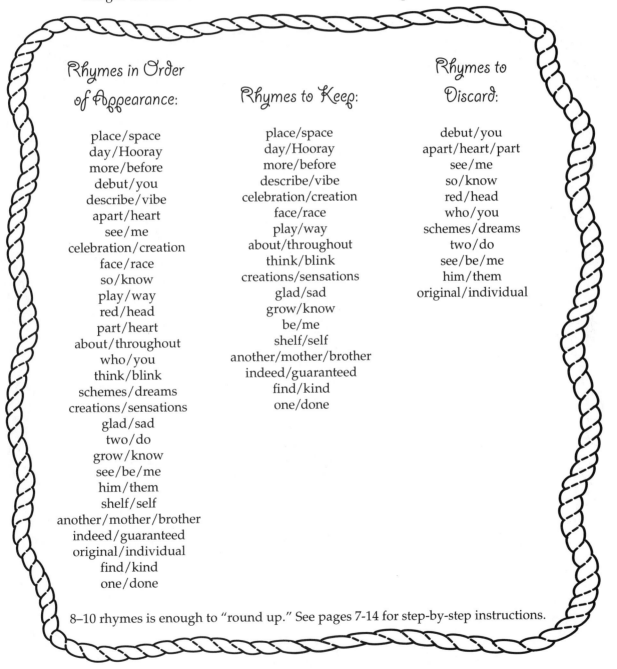

Rhymes in Order of Appearance:

place/space
day/Hooray
more/before
debut/you
describe/vibe
apart/heart
see/me
celebration/creation
face/race
so/know
play/way
red/head
part/heart
about/throughout
who/you
think/blink
schemes/dreams
creations/sensations
glad/sad
two/do
grow/know
see/be/me
him/them
shelf/self
another/mother/brother
indeed/guaranteed
original/individual
find/kind
one/done

Rhymes to Keep:

place/space
day/Hooray
more/before
describe/vibe
celebration/creation
face/race
play/way
about/throughout
think/blink
creations/sensations
glad/sad
grow/know
be/me
shelf/self
another/mother/brother
indeed/guaranteed
find/kind
one/done

Rhymes to Discard:

debut/you
apart/heart/part
see/me
so/know
red/head
who/you
schemes/dreams
two/do
see/be/me
him/them
original/individual

8–10 rhymes is enough to "round up." See pages 7-14 for step-by-step instructions.

Rounding Up the Rhymes • Grades 1–3

House Mouse, Senate Mouse

by Peter W. and Cheryl Shaw Barnes (Rosebud Books, 1996)

ISBN 0-9637688-4-0

Summary: The United Mice of America have their own Capitol. There, proposed laws are debated and passed or defeated. This delightful parody helps children understand the legislative branch of our government and how laws are enacted.

Rhymes in Order of Appearance:

too/who
will/Hill
own/stone
detail/nail
state/eight
straight/late
better/letter
soon/noon
read/said
please/cheese
pass/class
A/day
crates/states
McMouse/House
Senate/Bennett
blink/think
back/track
bill/skill
begin/within
bill/until
more/floor
House/Congressmouse
do/too
agree/be
Cheese/unease
spot/not
less/mess
bleaker/Squeaker
Hill/bill
meet/feet
years/ears
wise/compromise
Constitution/solution
small/all
please/Cheese
twice/advice
away/day

Rhymes to Keep:

will/Hill
detail/nail
better/letter
soon/noon
pass/class
crates/states
McMouse/House
blink/think
back/track
bill/skill
begin/within
House/Congressmouse
spot/not
less/mess
bleaker/Squeaker
Hill/bill
meet/feet
years/ears
wise/compromise
Constitution/solution
small/all
twice/advice
away/day

Rhymes to Discard:

too/who
own/stone
state/eight/straight/late
read/said
please/cheese
A/day
Senate/Bennett
bill/until
more/floor
do/too
agree/be
Cheese/unease

8–10 rhymes is enough to "round up." See pages 7-14 for step-by-step instructions.

How I Spent My Summer Vacation

by Mark Teague (Dragonfly Books, 1997)

ISBN 0-51788-556-5

Summary: Wallace Bleff shares a report about his summer vacation with his class, adding in his own imaginative details.

Rhymes in Order of Appearance:	Rhymes to Keep:	Rhymes to Discard:
west/rest	west/rest	crowd/loud
crowd/loud	sit/quit	said/instead
said/instead	say/okay	clothes/toes
sit/quit	hat/that	through/you
say/okay	tricks/sticks	me/tree
clothes/toes	land/cowhand	
hat/that	day/way	
tricks/sticks	eat/beat	
land/cowhand	sight/fright	
through/you	day/say	
day/way	ground/around	
eat/beat	display/away	
sight/fright	buckaroo/too	
day/say		
me/tree		
ground/around		
display/away		
buckaroo/too		

8–10 rhymes is enough to "round up." See pages 7-14 for step-by-step instructions.

45

How Many, How Many, How Many

by Rick Walton (Candlewick Press, 1996)

ISBN 1-56402-656-6

Summary: This book, in addition to being a counting book, is also an introduction to seasons, months of the year, nursery rhyme characters, and planets.

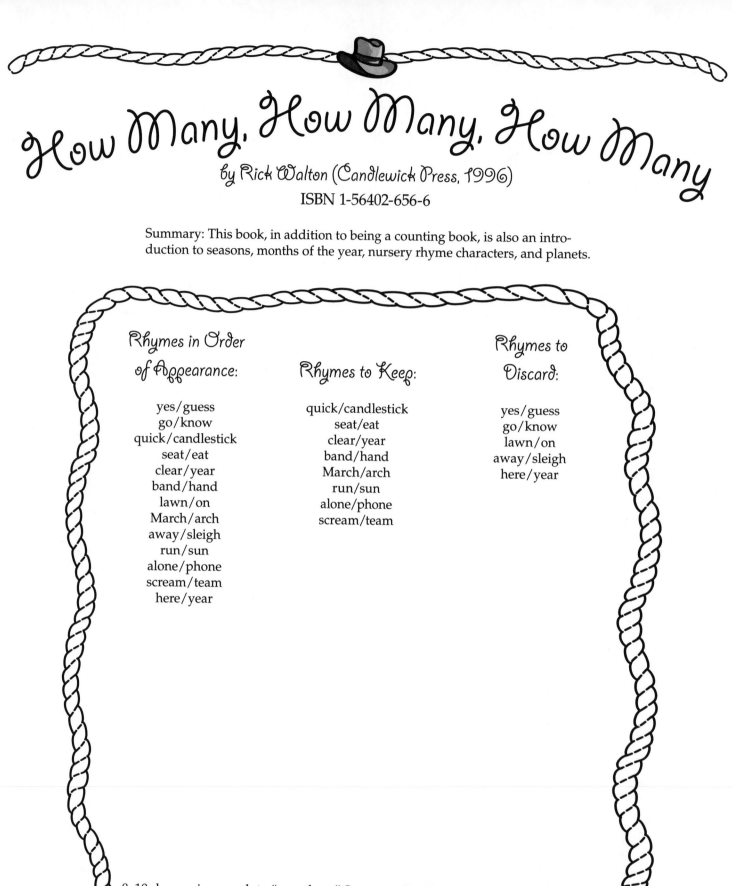

Rhymes in Order of Appearance:

yes/guess
go/know
quick/candlestick
seat/eat
clear/year
band/hand
lawn/on
March/arch
away/sleigh
run/sun
alone/phone
scream/team
here/year

Rhymes to Keep:

quick/candlestick
seat/eat
clear/year
band/hand
March/arch
run/sun
alone/phone
scream/team

Rhymes to Discard:

yes/guess
go/know
lawn/on
away/sleigh
here/year

8–10 rhymes is enough to "round up." See pages 7-14 for step-by-step instructions.

I Love Words

by Barbara Barbieri McGrath (Charlesbridge Publishing, 2003)

ISBN 1-57091-568-7

Summary: Heart candies with words written on them are used to encourage young readers. This text features sight words, rhyming words, question words, compound words, contractions, and opposites.

Rhymes in Order of Appearance:

now/how
Z/see
sound/around
heard/word
my/Y
say/way
try/why
might/sight
we/me
spell/tell
more/for
look/book
then/When
ten/again
white/right
do/blue
one/done
won't/don't
fun/one
rainbow/know
rhyme/time
make/cake
book/look
see/me/tree
jump/bump
big/pig
he/knee/three
hop/pop
box/fox
go/no/grow

feet/meet
ring/sing
low/tow/show
same/game
go/no
grin/thin
snake/make
hiss/this
while/smile
friend/end

Rhymes to Keep:

now/how
sound/around
say/way
try/why
might/sight
we/me
spell/tell
look/book
then/When
one/done
won't/don't
rainbow/know
make/cake
book/look
see/tree
jump/bump
big/pig
knee/three
hop/pop
box/fox

go/no
feet/meet
ring/sing
low/tow/show
same/game
go/no
grin/thin
snake/make
while/smile

Rhymes to Discard:

Z/see
heard/word
my/Y
A/say
more/for
ten/again
white/right
do/blue
fun/one
rhyme/time
me
he
grow
hiss/this
friend/end

8–10 rhymes is enough to "round up." See pages 7-14 for step-by-step instructions.

Rounding Up the Rhymes • Grades 1–3

I Love You Because You're You

by Liza Baker (Cartwheel Books, 2001)

ISBN 0-43920-638-3

Summary: A mother's love for her child endures even through many different situations in life.

Rhymes in Order of Appearance:

ear/near
'round/sound
knee/flee
there/air
bed/head
hug/rug
pout/shout
do/you

Rhymes to Keep:

ear/near
'round/sound
knee/flee
hug/rug
pout/shout

Rhymes to Discard:

there/air
bed/head
do/you

See pages 7-14 for step-by-step instructions.

I Love You, Mom

by Iris Hiskey Arno (Troll Communications, 2000)

ISBN 0-81674-440-8

Summary: Children tell of their mothers' different occupations and how they fit their families into busy schedules.

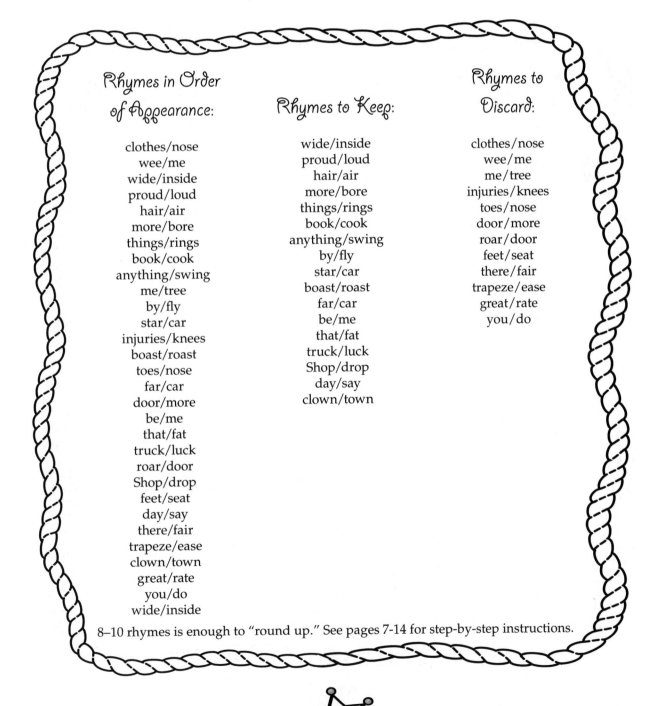

Rhymes in Order of Appearance:

clothes/nose
wee/me
wide/inside
proud/loud
hair/air
more/bore
things/rings
book/cook
anything/swing
me/tree
by/fly
star/car
injuries/knees
boast/roast
toes/nose
far/car
door/more
be/me
that/fat
truck/luck
roar/door
Shop/drop
feet/seat
day/say
there/fair
trapeze/ease
clown/town
great/rate
you/do
wide/inside

Rhymes to Keep:

wide/inside
proud/loud
hair/air
more/bore
things/rings
book/cook
anything/swing
by/fly
star/car
boast/roast
far/car
be/me
that/fat
truck/luck
Shop/drop
day/say
clown/town

Rhymes to Discard:

clothes/nose
wee/me
me/tree
injuries/knees
toes/nose
door/more
roar/door
feet/seat
there/fair
trapeze/ease
great/rate
you/do

8–10 rhymes is enough to "round up." See pages 7-14 for step-by-step instructions.

Rounding Up the Rhymes • Grades 1–3

If I Ran the Rain Forest

by Bonnie Worth (Random House Books for Young Readers, 2003)

ISBN 0-375-81097-8

Summary: Take a trip to the rainforest with the Cat in the Hat. Throughout the adventure you will learn many interesting facts in a fun rhyming rhythm.

Rhymes in Order of Appearance:

get/wet
clear/year
you/do
go/know
dry/high
coast/most
information/transpiration
say/way
view/you
call/tall
report/support
fan/plan
best/nest
hue/blue
three/canopy
below/grow
there/air
spots/lots
flowers/hours
found/ground
tricky/sticky
hum/sum
blooms/zooms
grow/so
head/spread
ride/inside
another/smother
two/through
hot/ocelot
prize/eyes
wide/outside
not/rot
slither/hither
find/humankind
unharmed/farmed
meal/heal
them/ecosystem
years/tears
year/here
do/do
trees/please

Rhymes to Keep:

get/wet
clear/year
information/transpiration
say/way
call/tall
report/support
fan/plan
best/nest
hue/blue
below/grow
spots/lots
found/ground
tricky/sticky
hum/sum
blooms/zooms
head/spread
ride/inside
another/smother
hot/ocelot
wide/outside

not/rot
slither/hither
find/humankind
unharmed/farmed
meal/heal
them/ecosystem
years/tears

Rhymes to Discard:

you/do
go/know
dry/high
coast/most
view/you
three/canopy
there/air
flowers/hours
grow/so
two/through
prize/eyes
year/here
do/do
trees/please

8–10 rhymes is enough to "round up." See pages 7-14 for step-by-step instructions.

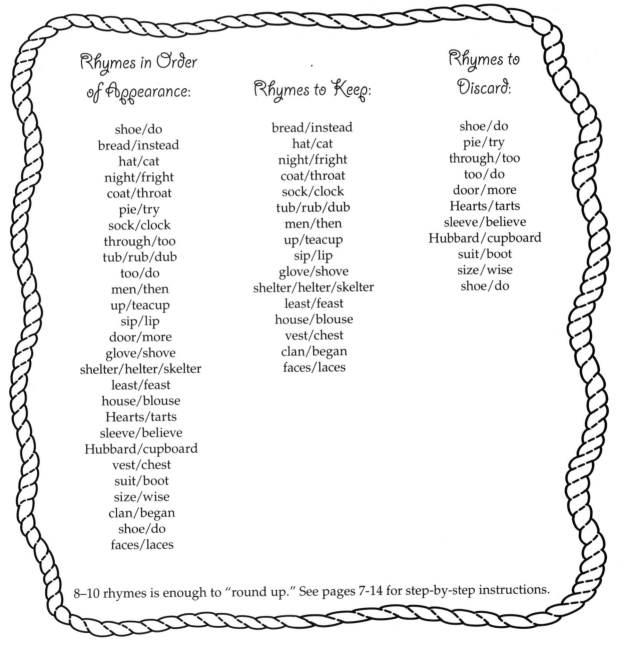

If the Shoe Fits

by Alison Jackson (Henry Holt and Co., 2001)

ISBN 0-80506-466-4

Summary: The old woman who lived in a shoe decides she and her family have outgrown their "house." She takes them to try out several new residences where they are met by a bevy of nursery rhyme characters. Eventually, the old woman comes back to the shoe, which she now decides is just right for her family.

Rhymes in Order of Appearance:	Rhymes to Keep:	Rhymes to Discard:
shoe/do	bread/instead	shoe/do
bread/instead	hat/cat	pie/try
hat/cat	night/fright	through/too
night/fright	coat/throat	too/do
coat/throat	sock/clock	door/more
pie/try	tub/rub/dub	Hearts/tarts
sock/clock	men/then	sleeve/believe
through/too	up/teacup	Hubbard/cupboard
tub/rub/dub	sip/lip	suit/boot
too/do	glove/shove	size/wise
men/then	shelter/helter/skelter	shoe/do
up/teacup	least/feast	
sip/lip	house/blouse	
door/more	vest/chest	
glove/shove	clan/began	
shelter/helter/skelter	faces/laces	
least/feast		
house/blouse		
Hearts/tarts		
sleeve/believe		
Hubbard/cupboard		
vest/chest		
suit/boot		
size/wise		
clan/began		
shoe/do		
faces/laces		

8–10 rhymes is enough to "round up." See pages 7-14 for step-by-step instructions.

I'll Teach My Dog 100 Words

by Michael Frith (HarperCollins, 1983)

ISBN 0-00171-277-2

Summary: Everyone in town is amazed as the smartest dog learns 100 words, or so they think. Follow the antics of this new pup as he encounters his learning experiences.

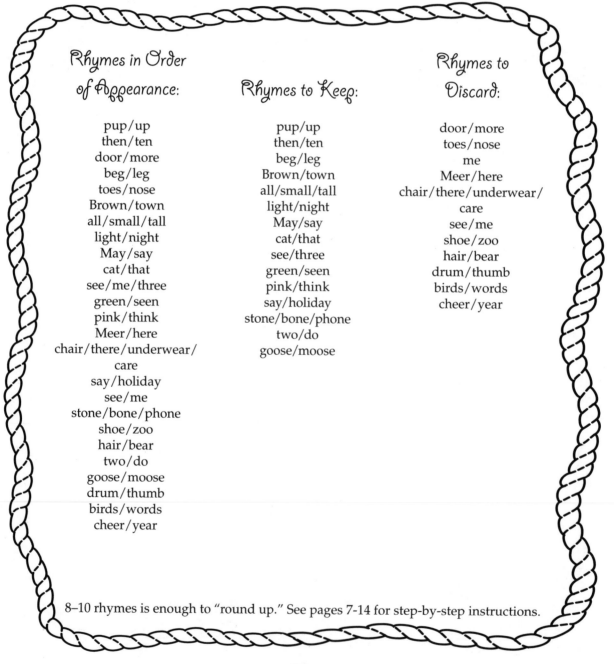

Rhymes in Order of Appearance:

pup/up
then/ten
door/more
beg/leg
toes/nose
Brown/town
all/small/tall
light/night
May/say
cat/that
see/me/three
green/seen
pink/think
Meer/here
chair/there/underwear/
care
say/holiday
see/me
stone/bone/phone
shoe/zoo
hair/bear
two/do
goose/moose
drum/thumb
birds/words
cheer/year

Rhymes to Keep:

pup/up
then/ten
beg/leg
Brown/town
all/small/tall
light/night
May/say
cat/that
see/three
green/seen
pink/think
say/holiday
stone/bone/phone
two/do
goose/moose

Rhymes to Discard:

door/more
toes/nose
me
Meer/here
chair/there/underwear/
care
see/me
shoe/zoo
hair/bear
drum/thumb
birds/words
cheer/year

8–10 rhymes is enough to "round up." See pages 7-14 for step-by-step instructions.

52

In 1492

by Jean Marzollo (Scholastic, 1993)

ISBN 0-59044-414-X

Summary: This fun rhyming book will take children across the seas with Christopher Columbus and allow them to share in his adventures.

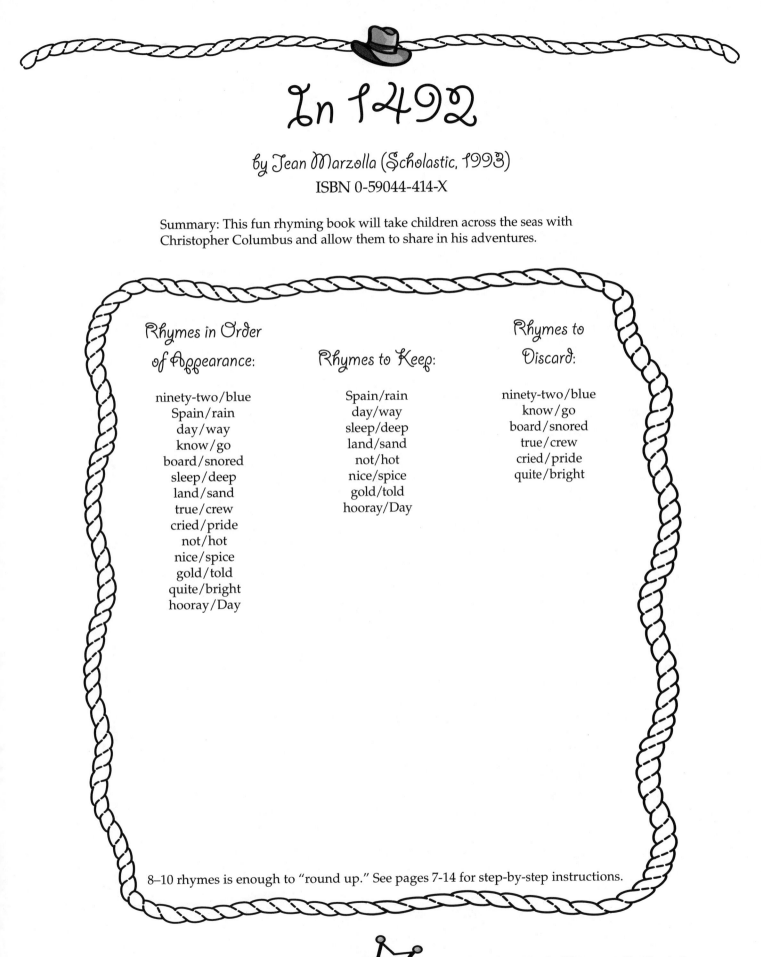

Rhymes in Order of Appearance:

ninety-two/blue
Spain/rain
day/way
know/go
board/snored
sleep/deep
land/sand
true/crew
cried/pride
not/hot
nice/spice
gold/told
quite/bright
hooray/Day

Rhymes to Keep:

Spain/rain
day/way
sleep/deep
land/sand
not/hot
nice/spice
gold/told
hooray/Day

Rhymes to Discard:

ninety-two/blue
know/go
board/snored
true/crew
cried/pride
quite/bright

8–10 rhymes is enough to "round up." See pages 7-14 for step-by-step instructions.

Inchworm and a Half

by Elinor J. Pinczes (Houghton Mifflin, 2003)

ISBN 0-61831-101-7

Summary: Small worms use their differing lengths to measure all of the vegetables in the garden. Fractions are enlisted when the vegetables don't fit the exact length of the inchworm. Fractions of $1/8$, $1/3$, and $1/4$ are used to help measure accurately.

Rhymes in Order of Appearance:	Rhymes to Keep:	Rhymes to Discard:
ease/peas	measures/treasures	ease/peas
measures/treasures	inch/cinch	beans/greens
inch/cinch	end/depend	three/be
end/depend	hoop/loop	air/there
hoop/loop	bit/fit	worm/squirm
beans/greens	number/cucumber	fun/done
bit/fit	One/done	me/see
three/be	ears/spears	wise/size
air/there	two/do	laugh/half
worm/squirm	wrong/along	occurred/third
number/cucumber	me/be	head/red
fun/done	spot/dot	few/do
me/see	try/spry	agree/be
wise/size	twice/nice	absurd/third
laugh/half	before/more	curled/world
One/done	small/all	
ears/spears		
two/do		
wrong/along		
me/be		
spot/dot		
try/spry		
occurred/third		
head/red		
twice/nice		
few/do		
before/more		
agree/be		
absurd/third		
curled/world		
small/all		

8–10 rhymes is enough to "round up." See pages 7-14 for step-by-step instructions.

Itchy, Itchy Chicken Pox

by Grace MacCarone (Scholastic, 1992)

ISBN 0-59044-948-6

Summary: Oh, no! The little boy is breaking out in spots all over his body. This book helps children understand how to deal with the discomforts of chicken pox.

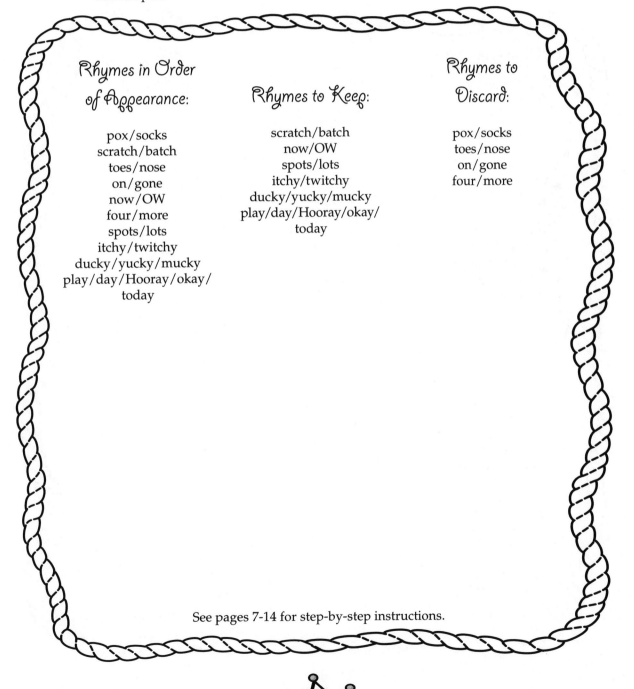

Rhymes in Order of Appearance:

pox/socks
scratch/batch
toes/nose
on/gone
now/OW
four/more
spots/lots
itchy/twitchy
ducky/yucky/mucky
play/day/Hooray/okay/
today

Rhymes to Keep:

scratch/batch
now/OW
spots/lots
itchy/twitchy
ducky/yucky/mucky
play/day/Hooray/okay/
today

Rhymes to Discard:

pox/socks
toes/nose
on/gone
four/more

See pages 7-14 for step-by-step instructions.

It's St. Patrick's Day!

by Rebecca Gomez (Cartwheel Books, 2004)

ISBN 0-43944-160-9

Summary: Children celebrate St. Patrick's Day with tradition and lots of fun.

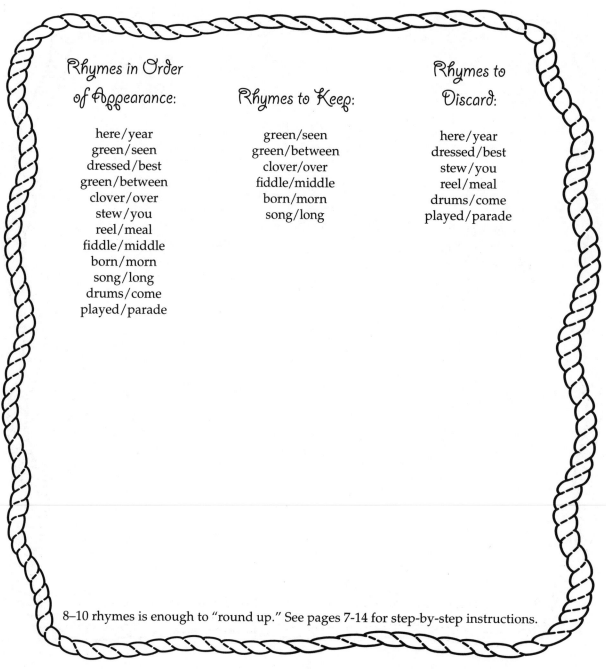

Rhymes in Order of Appearance:

here/year
green/seen
dressed/best
green/between
clover/over
stew/you
reel/meal
fiddle/middle
born/morn
song/long
drums/come
played/parade

Rhymes to Keep:

green/seen
green/between
clover/over
fiddle/middle
born/morn
song/long

Rhymes to Discard:

here/year
dressed/best
stew/you
reel/meal
drums/come
played/parade

8–10 rhymes is enough to "round up." See pages 7-14 for step-by-step instructions.

56

Jennifer Jones Won't Leave Me Alone

by Frieda Wishinsky (HarperCollins, 1997)
ISBN 0-00648-072-1

Summary: Jennifer Jones has a crush on a boy in her class. The other students make fun of the two, and the boy wishes that she would move away. When Jennifer Jones does move, he finds that he misses her and wishes for her return.

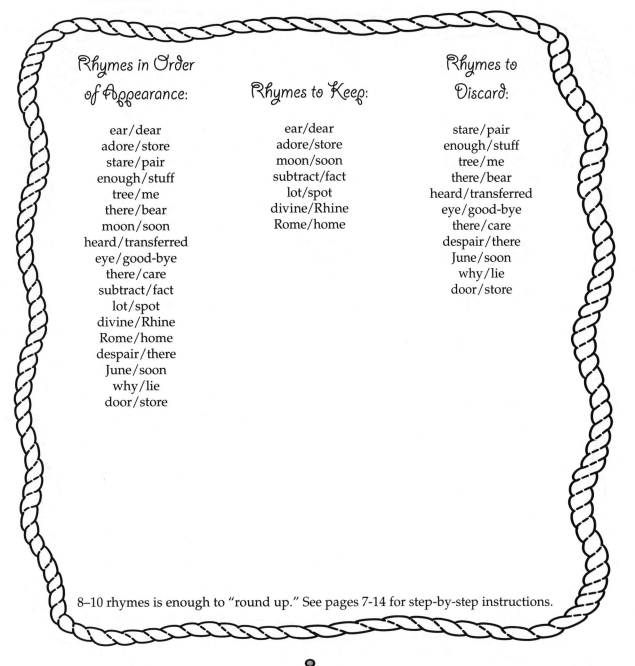

Rhymes in Order of Appearance:

ear/dear
adore/store
stare/pair
enough/stuff
tree/me
there/bear
moon/soon
heard/transferred
eye/good-bye
there/care
subtract/fact
lot/spot
divine/Rhine
Rome/home
despair/there
June/soon
why/lie
door/store

Rhymes to Keep:

ear/dear
adore/store
moon/soon
subtract/fact
lot/spot
divine/Rhine
Rome/home

Rhymes to Discard:

stare/pair
enough/stuff
tree/me
there/bear
heard/transferred
eye/good-bye
there/care
despair/there
June/soon
why/lie
door/store

8–10 rhymes is enough to "round up." See pages 7-14 for step-by-step instructions.

57

Rounding Up the Rhymes • Grades 1–3

The Library

by Sarah Stewart (Farrar, Straus and Giroux, 1999)

ISBN 0-37444-394-7

Summary: Elizabeth Brown loves to read more than anything else. She surrounds herself with as many books as she can. Eventually, she owns more books than her house will hold. She thinks of a splendid solution to this problem.

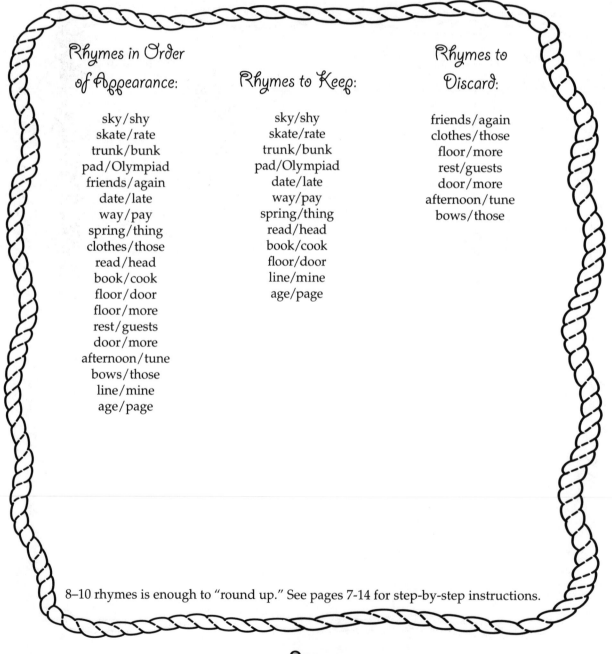

Rhymes in Order of Appearance:

sky/shy
skate/rate
trunk/bunk
pad/Olympiad
friends/again
date/late
way/pay
spring/thing
clothes/those
read/head
book/cook
floor/door
floor/more
rest/guests
door/more
afternoon/tune
bows/those
line/mine
age/page

Rhymes to Keep:

sky/shy
skate/rate
trunk/bunk
pad/Olympiad
date/late
way/pay
spring/thing
read/head
book/cook
floor/door
line/mine
age/page

Rhymes to Discard:

friends/again
clothes/those
floor/more
rest/guests
door/more
afternoon/tune
bows/those

8–10 rhymes is enough to "round up." See pages 7-14 for step-by-step instructions.

Little Miss Spider

by David Kirk (Scholastic Press, 2003)

ISBN 0-43954-315-0

Summary: Little Miss Spider has just popped out of her egg and discovers that she can't find her mother anywhere. In her search for her mom, she encounters many dangers but, eventually, discovers the true meaning of motherhood.

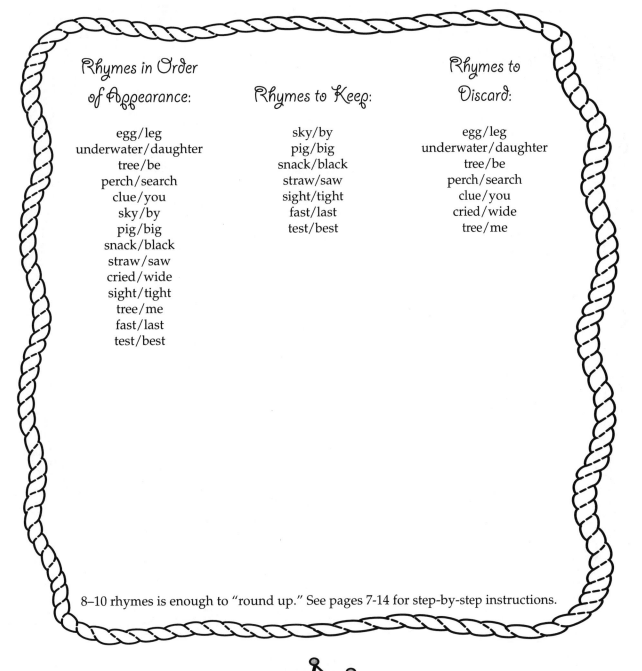

Rhymes in Order of Appearance:	Rhymes to Keep:	Rhymes to Discard:
egg/leg	sky/by	egg/leg
underwater/daughter	pig/big	underwater/daughter
tree/be	snack/black	tree/be
perch/search	straw/saw	perch/search
clue/you	sight/tight	clue/you
sky/by	fast/last	cried/wide
pig/big	test/best	tree/me
snack/black		
straw/saw		
cried/wide		
sight/tight		
tree/me		
fast/last		
test/best		

8–10 rhymes is enough to "round up." See pages 7-14 for step-by-step instructions.

Lizards for Lunch

by Conrad J. Storad (RGU Group, 2002)

ISBN 1-89179-500-7

Summary: Learn about roadrunners and their characteristics in this fun-loving, illustrated book.

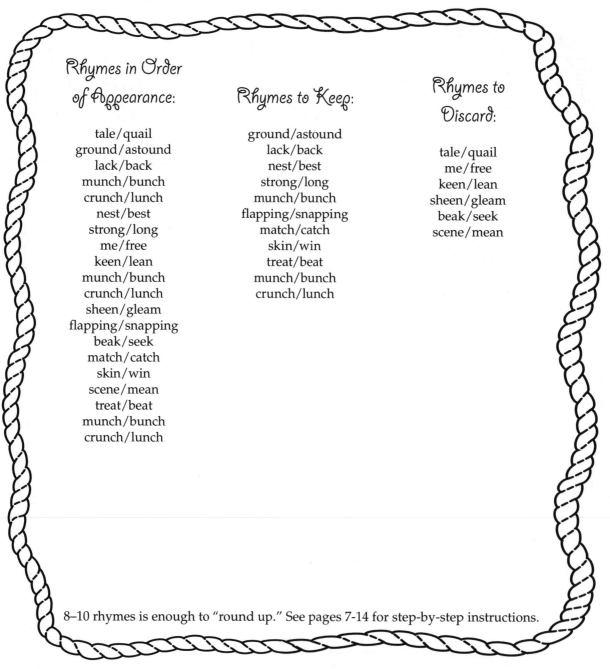

Rhymes in Order of Appearance:

tale/quail
ground/astound
lack/back
munch/bunch
crunch/lunch
nest/best
strong/long
me/free
keen/lean
munch/bunch
crunch/lunch
sheen/gleam
flapping/snapping
beak/seek
match/catch
skin/win
scene/mean
treat/beat
munch/bunch
crunch/lunch

Rhymes to Keep:

ground/astound
lack/back
nest/best
strong/long
munch/bunch
flapping/snapping
match/catch
skin/win
treat/beat
munch/bunch
crunch/lunch

Rhymes to Discard:

tale/quail
me/free
keen/lean
sheen/gleam
beak/seek
scene/mean

8–10 rhymes is enough to "round up." See pages 7-14 for step-by-step instructions.

60

Loud Lips Lucy

by Tolya L. Thompson (Savor Publishing House, 2001)
ISBN 0-97082-960-4

Summary: Lucille Lucy is never quiet, which results in her missing out on the sounds around her. A case of laryngitis changes the way she sees the world and helps her to discover the importance of listening.

Rhymes in Order of Appearance:

her/holler
wide/inside
mouth/shout
say/way
hips/chips
that/chat
fall/all
scream/cream
proud/loud
day/way
name/same
right/tight
try/by
true/through
choice/voice
think/sink
dear/rear
look/book
ground/around
nose/toes
hair/there
be/me
pout/out
tree/me
sing/thing
clear/here
chirped/burped
sky/by
who/do/moo
lips/hips

floor/before
do/too
galore/more
be/me
happened/yappin'
around/sound
dark/park
fool/cool
find/mind

Rhymes to Keep:

her/holler
wide/inside
say/way
hips/chips
that/chat
fall/all
scream/cream
proud/loud
day/way
name/same
right/tight
try/by
choice/voice
think/sink
dear/rear
look/book
ground/around
be/me
pout/out
sing/thing
sky/by
lips/hips

galore/more
be/me
around/sound
dark/park
fool/cool
find/mind

Rhymes to Discard:

mouth/shout
true/through
nose/toes
hair/there
tree/me
clear/here
chirped/burped
who/do/moo
floor/before
do/too
happened/yappin'

8–10 rhymes is enough to "round up." See pages 7-14 for step-by-step instructions.

The M&M's® Brand Color Pattern Book

by Barbara Barbieri McGrath (Charlesbridge Publishing, 2002)

ISBN 1-57091-417-6

Summary: Children can learn about colors and patterns with this hands-on M&M's® Brand book.

Rhymes in Order of Appearance:

candy/handy
six/mix
blue/too
choose/use
line/fine
fit/it
sight/right
then/again
repeat/eat
more/twenty-four
do/blue
down/brown
eighteen/green
in/begin
do/blue
see/three
row/go
three/agree
new/two
try/my
count/amount
nod/odd
book/look
these/please
done/one
wait/celebrate

Rhymes to Keep:

candy/handy
six/mix
line/fine
fit/it
sight/right
repeat/eat
down/brown
eighteen/green
in/begin
see/three
three/agree
try/my
count/amount
book/look
done/one

Rhymes to Discard:

blue/too
choose/use
then/again
more/twenty-four
do/blue
row/go
new/two
nod/odd
these/please
wait/celebrate

8–10 rhymes is enough to "round up." See pages 7-14 for step-by-step instructions.

The M&M's® Brand Counting Book

by Barbara Barbieri McGrath (Charlesbridge Publishing, 1994)

ISBN 0-88106-853-5

Summary: Children can enjoy learning about counting, colors, shapes, sets, and subtraction with this fun M&M's® Brand book.

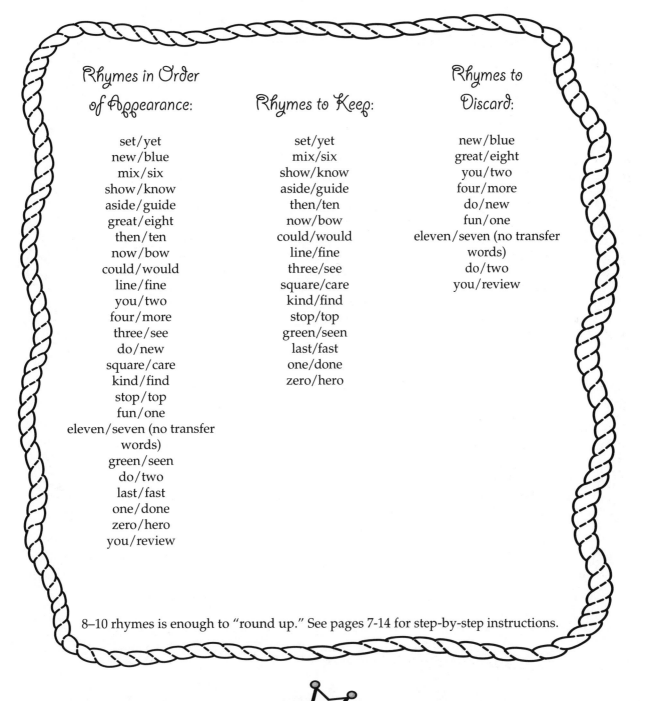

Rhymes in Order of Appearance:

set/yet
new/blue
mix/six
show/know
aside/guide
great/eight
then/ten
now/bow
could/would
line/fine
you/two
four/more
three/see
do/new
square/care
kind/find
stop/top
fun/one
eleven/seven (no transfer words)
green/seen
do/two
last/fast
one/done
zero/hero
you/review

Rhymes to Keep:

set/yet
mix/six
show/know
aside/guide
then/ten
now/bow
could/would
line/fine
three/see
square/care
kind/find
stop/top
green/seen
last/fast
one/done
zero/hero

Rhymes to Discard:

new/blue
great/eight
you/two
four/more
do/new
fun/one
eleven/seven (no transfer words)
do/two
you/review

8–10 rhymes is enough to "round up." See pages 7-14 for step-by-step instructions.

Many Luscious Lollipops

by Ruth Heller (Putnam Publishing Group, 1998)

ISBN 0-69811-641-0

Summary: Colorful illustrations and vivid examples give children delightful insight into the various kinds of adjectives and their functions.

Rhymes in Order of Appearance:

terrific/specific
identifies/size/butterflies
grace/place/space/race/ace
emotion/notion
gumdrops/lollipops
fails/details
say/display
before/more
day/gray/okay/way
blue/do/too
choose/shoes/whose/
news
nose/pose/toes
gait/mate
the/see/balcony
setter/letter
crown/gown
dress/Bess
pearls/curls
compare/fair
best/rest
more/four
least/beast/feast

Rhymes to Keep:

terrific/specific
identifies/butterflies
grace/place/space/race/ace
emotion/notion
gumdrops/lollipops
fails/details
say/display
before/more
day/gray/okay/way
nose/pose
setter/letter
crown/gown
dress/Bess
best/rest
least/beast/feast

Rhymes to Discard:

size
blue/do/too
choose/shoes/whose/
news
toes
gait/mate
the/see/balcony
pearls/curls
compare/fair
more/four

8–10 rhymes is enough to "round up." See pages 7-14 for step-by-step instructions.

Marshall, the Courthouse Mouse

by Peter W. and Cheryl Shaw Barnes (Rosebud Books, 1998)

ISBN 0-96376-886-7

Summary: The mice have a Supreme Court, just like humans. In this story, the Supreme Court of the United Mice of America must decide a very difficult case. This book helps children understand our nation's Supreme Court and how the laws of our land are adjudicated.

Rhymes in Order of Appearance:

near/cheer
report/Court
mice/nice
contribution/Constitution
sleeve/believe
one/done
around/underground
charge/large
there/fair
obey/day
bike/like
steal/automobile
school/rule
nights/Rights
vote/note
decide/pride
hear/unclear
unusual/Un-Constitutional
created/stated
day/obey
Cheddar/better
Mozzarella/fella
plate/ate
supreme/Cream
along/wrong
able/table
good/should
support/Court
tradition/petition
address/less
small/all
start/smart
view/too
decide/provide
fall/all
said/ahead
looks/books
dash/flash
chair/everywhere
months/once
table/able
solution/constitution
right/appetite
meal/feel
see/Constitutionally
agree/unani-mouse-ly
next/text
agreed/read
decision/precision
declaration/nation
wide/abide
understand/land
everywhere/share
support/Court
created/stated

Rhymes to Keep:

mice/nice
contribution/Constitution
one/done
around/underground
charge/large
bike/like
nights/Rights
vote/note
decide/pride
hear/unclear
Mozzarella/fella
plate/ate
along/wrong
able/table
tradition/petition
address/less
small/all
start/smart
decide/provide
fall/all
looks/books
dash/flash
table/able
solution/constitution
next/text
decision/precision
declaration/nation
wide/abide
understand/land

8–10 rhymes is enough to "round up." See pages 7-14 for step-by-step instructions.

Rhymes to
Discard:

near/cheer
report/Court
sleeve/believe
there/fair
obey/day
steal/automobile
school/rule
unusual/Un-Constitutional
day/obey
Cheddar/better
supreme/Cream
good/should
support/Court
view/too
said/ahead
chair/everywhere
months/once
right/appetite
meal/feel
see/Constitutionally
agree/unani-mouse-ly
agreed/read
everywhere/share
support/Court

A Mink, a Fink, a Skating Rink

by Brian P. Cleary (Carolrhoda Books, Inc., 1999)

ISBN 1-57505-402-7

Summary: Nouns are everywhere. See examples of the many nouns that surround us in this book, which combines rhymes and illustrations to help children easily identify nouns.

Rhymes in Order of Appearance:

Mink/Fink/Rink
Hill/Mill/Phil
Gown/noun/crown/hometown
deer/chandelier
train/brain
frown/noun
proper/Hopper
Pekinese/these
jail/nail/bale
hay/play
quarter/porter
pear/everywhere
lip/chip/sip
cuff/stuff
mink/fink/rink/sink
cake/rake
pope/soap/rope/slope
house/mouse
clock/sock
tar/bar/star/car
Lynn/in
jokes/folks
collar/scholar
sand/band
saxes/faxes
cat/bat/hat/that
town/noun
poodle/strudel/noodle
gasoline/machine/queen
thing/ring
boat/coat
clown/noun

Rhymes to Keep:

Mink/Fink/Rink
Hill/Mill
Gown/crown/hometown
train/brain
Pekinese/these
jail/nail
hay/play
lip/chip/sip
cuff/stuff
mink/fink/rink/sink
cake/rake
pope/rope/slope
house/mouse
clock/sock
tar/bar/star/car
sand/band
saxes/faxes
cat/bat/hat/that
poodle/noodle
gasoline/machine
thing/ring
boat/coat

Rhymes to Discard:

Phil
noun
dear/chandelier
frown/noun
proper/Hopper
bale
quarter/porter
pear/everywhere
soap
Lynn/in
jokes/folks
collar/scholar
town/noun
strudel
queen
clown/noun

8–10 rhymes is enough to "round up." See pages 7-14 for step-by-step instructions.

67

Miss Spider's New Car

by David Kirk (Scholastic Press, 1997)

ISBN 0-590-30713-4

Summary: Miss Spider and Holley decide that they need a car to go visit their mother. They find a car but hesitate to buy the first one that they find. After shopping around, they return to their first choice only to find that it is gone.

Rhymes in Order of Appearance:

cried/riverside/guide
frog/bog
mice/entice
snakes/shakes/sakes
far/car
divine/shine/fine
shells/bells
there/declare
frowned/found/around
bee/three
flower/power/hour
going/knowing/blowing
Escargo/slow/know
dinosaur/for/roar
brown/down
brings/things/wings
holes/moles
run/one/done
dream/schemed
bump/pump/jump
three/secretly/me
Sue/do
cried/replied/sighed
ma'am/am
sight/might/right
Sue/through
door/floor
note/wrote/boat

Rhymes to Keep:

frog/bog
mice/entice
snakes/shakes/sakes
far/car
divine/shine/fine
shells/bells
found/around
bee/three
flower/power
knowing/blowing
slow/know
brown/down
brings/things/wings
holes/moles
one/done
bump/pump/jump
cried/replied
ma'am/am
sight/might/right
door/floor
note/wrote

Rhymes to Discard:

cried/riverside/guide
there/declare
frowned
hour
going
Escargo
dinosaur/for/roar
run
dream/schemed
three/secretly/me
Sue/do
sighed
Sue/through
boat

8–10 rhymes is enough to "round up." See pages 7-14 for step-by-step instructions.

More M&M's® Brand Math

by Barbara Barbieri McGrath (Charlesbridge Publishing, 1998)

ISBN 0-88106-994-9

Summary: Using M&M's® Brand Chocolate Candies, children will learn about guessing, sorting, graphing, and comparing.

Rhymes in Order of Appearance:	Rhymes to Keep:	Rhymes to Discard:
tools/rules	get/yet	tools/rules
get/yet	candy/handy	blue/too
candy/handy	pile/while	ceased/least
pile/while	tall/call	two/you
blue/too	show/low	see/carefully
ceased/least	grand/hand	true/two
tall/call	treat/eat	again/ten
show/low	guide/divide	eight/great
grand/hand	done/one	clear/here
treat/eat	bunch/munch	more/four
guide/divide	plenty/twenty	use/choose
two/you	line/fine	word/third
done/one	path/math	passed/last
bunch/munch		
see/carefully		
true/two		
again/ten		
eight/great		
clear/here		
plenty/twenty		
more/four		
line/fine		
use/choose		
word/third		
passed/last		
path/math		

8–10 rhymes is enough to "round up." See pages 7-14 for step-by-step instructions.

Rounding Up the Rhymes • Grades 1–3

More Parts

by Tedd Arnold (Puffin Books, 2003)

ISBN 0-14250-149-2

Summary: A little boy is very concerned about the expressions he hears in the everyday speech of his family and friends. He takes very literally the figures of speech that make it sound as if his body parts may not be so firmly in place. Finally, Mom and Dad are able to quiet his fears.

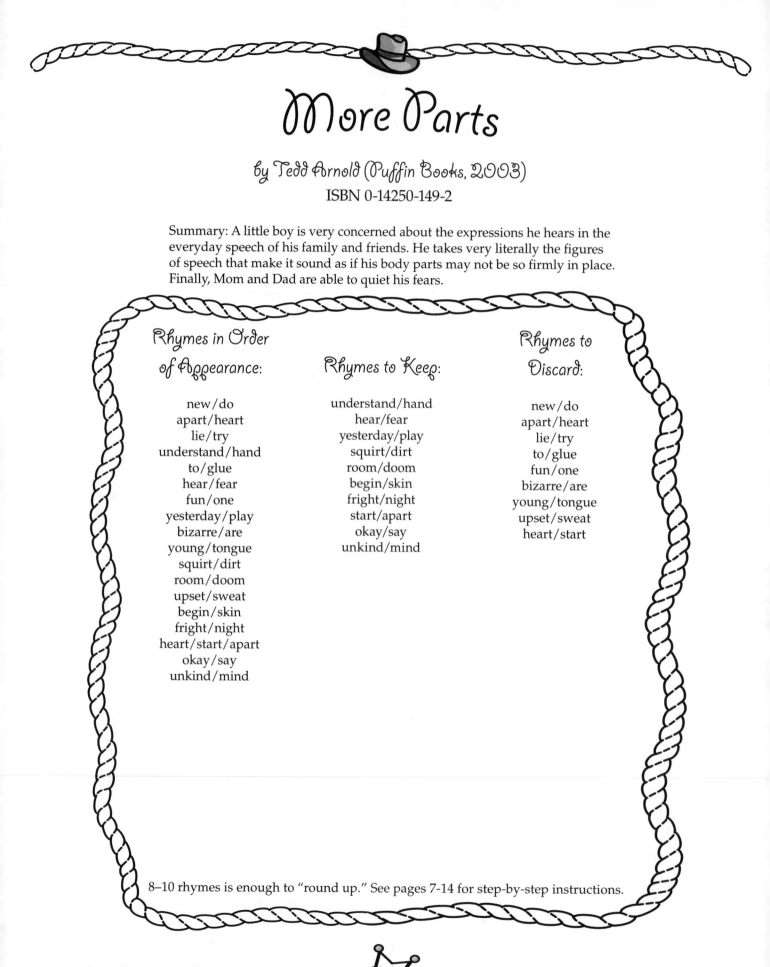

Rhymes in Order of Appearance:

new/do
apart/heart
lie/try
understand/hand
to/glue
hear/fear
fun/one
yesterday/play
bizarre/are
young/tongue
squirt/dirt
room/doom
upset/sweat
begin/skin
fright/night
heart/start/apart
okay/say
unkind/mind

Rhymes to Keep:

understand/hand
hear/fear
yesterday/play
squirt/dirt
room/doom
begin/skin
fright/night
start/apart
okay/say
unkind/mind

Rhymes to Discard:

new/do
apart/heart
lie/try
to/glue
fun/one
bizarre/are
young/tongue
upset/sweat
heart/start

8–10 rhymes is enough to "round up." See pages 7-14 for step-by-step instructions.

Motherlove

by Virginia Kroll (Dawn Publications, 1998)

ISBN 1-88322-080-7

Summary: Celebrate the love that mothers of all species bring to the challenges and joys of caring for their young. In addition to the lovely poetry, there is expository text about each of the mothers featured in the book.

Rhymes in Order of Appearance:

furry/purry
warm/storm
cuddle/huddle
space/place
upbringing/singing
sleep/cheep
preening/cleaning
eat/feet
slow/low
respecting/directing/
protecting
fly/why
hagglers/stragglers
strangers/dangers
cues/blues
pain/rain
cows/sows
more/shore
trees/seas
aunties/shanties
heave/leave
shoving/loving

Rhymes to Keep:

furry/purry
cuddle/huddle
space/place
upbringing/singing
sleep/cheep
slow/low
respecting/directing/
protecting
fly/why
hagglers/stragglers
strangers/dangers
cues/blues
pain/rain
cows/sows
more/shore
heave/leave
shoving/loving

Rhymes to Discard:

warm/storm
preening/cleaning
eat/feet
trees/seas
aunties/shanties

8–10 rhymes is enough to "round up." See pages 7-14 for step-by-step instructions.

The Mouse Before Christmas

by Michael Garland (Puffin Books, 2001)

ISBN 0-14230-005-5

Summary: A young mouse really wanted to see Santa, so he stayed awake late waiting for Santa's visit. Mouse hid so that he could see Santa stuff the stockings. He crept near Santa's bag and accidentally got bundled inside when Santa moved on to his next stop. After an exciting tour around the world, Santa discovered the mouse and flew him home.

Rhymes in Order of Appearance:

mouse/house
soul/hole
treat/eat
scurried/worried
sigh/high
quick/Nick
tumble/jumble
true/do
sag/bag
away/sleigh
inside/ride
shout/out
free/see
sky/fly
down/town
race/pace
river/aquiver
flew/view
land/grand
wide/ride
house/mouse
sea/Liberty
squeak/speak
ride/inside
worry/hurry
face/space
all/small
floor/door
bed/head
small/tall

Rhymes to Keep:

mouse/house
treat/eat
sigh/high
quick/Nick
tumble/jumble
sag/bag
inside/ride
shout/out
free/see
sky/fly
down/town
race/pace
river/aquiver
land/grand
wide/ride
house/mouse
squeak/speak
ride/inside
face/space
all/small
floor/door
small/tall

Rhymes to Discard:

eyes/wise
do/true/you

soul/hole
scurried/worried
true/do
away/sleigh
flew/view
sea/Liberty
worry/hurry
bed/head
eyes/wise
do/true/you

8–10 rhymes is enough to "round up." See pages 7-14 for step-by-step instructions.

Mr. Monopoly's Amusment Park

by Jackie Glassman (Scholastic, 2001)

ISBN 0-43931-792-4

Summary: This book encourages students to help the children in the story keep track of their money while enjoying a day at an amusement park. There are also more difficult questions included for children wanting a higher-level challenge.

Rhymes in Order of Appearance:	Rhymes to Keep:	Rhymes to Discard:
friends/spend	lot/spot	friends/spend
lot/spot	'round/ground	deal/wheel
deal/wheel	treat/eat	air/share
'round/ground	slide/ride	go/Show
treat/eat	splash/cash	hollers/dollars
air/share	Mars/cars	crowd/cloud
slide/ride	smack/pack	paid/arcade
splash/cash	rises/surprises	go/show
Mars/cars	most/ghost	
go/Show	chill/thrill	
hollers/dollars	end/spend	
crowd/cloud		
paid/arcade		
smack/pack		
go/show		
rises/surprises		
most/ghost		
chill/thrill		
end/spend		

8–10 rhymes is enough to "round up." See pages 7-14 for step-by-step instructions.

Mr. Wiggle's Book

by Paula Craig (Instructional Fair, 2001)

ISBN 1-56822-975-5

Summary: Mr. Wiggle is very sad because someone has abused his book in several different ways. He shares with readers how to take the best care of their books.

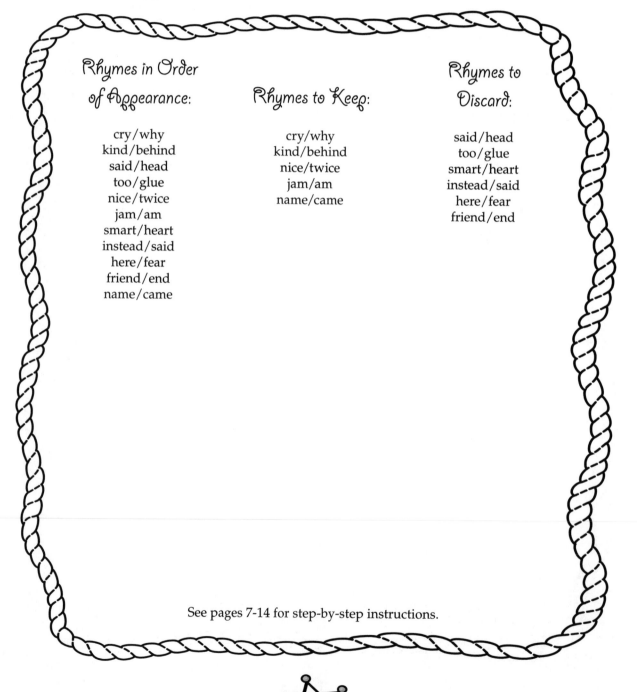

Rhymes in Order of Appearance:

cry/why
kind/behind
said/head
too/glue
nice/twice
jam/am
smart/heart
instead/said
here/fear
friend/end
name/came

Rhymes to Keep:

cry/why
kind/behind
nice/twice
jam/am
name/came

Rhymes to Discard:

said/head
too/glue
smart/heart
instead/said
here/fear
friend/end

See pages 7-14 for step-by-step instructions.

My Daddy and I

by P. K. Hallinan (Candy Cane Press, 2002)

ISBN 0-82494-217-5

Summary: This book is a celebration for dads from their children as different parent/child activities are shared.

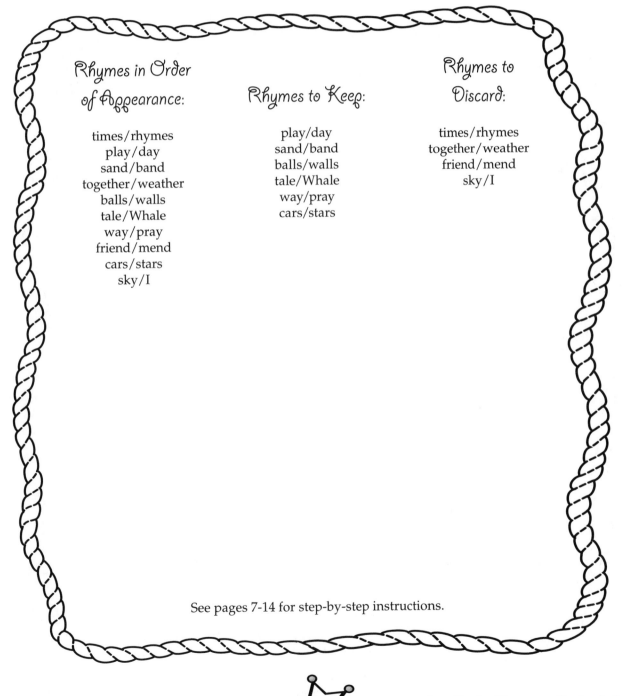

Rhymes in Order of Appearance:

times/rhymes
play/day
sand/band
together/weather
balls/walls
tale/Whale
way/pray
friend/mend
cars/stars
sky/I

Rhymes to Keep:

play/day
sand/band
balls/walls
tale/Whale
way/pray
cars/stars

Rhymes to Discard:

times/rhymes
together/weather
friend/mend
sky/I

See pages 7-14 for step-by-step instructions.

75

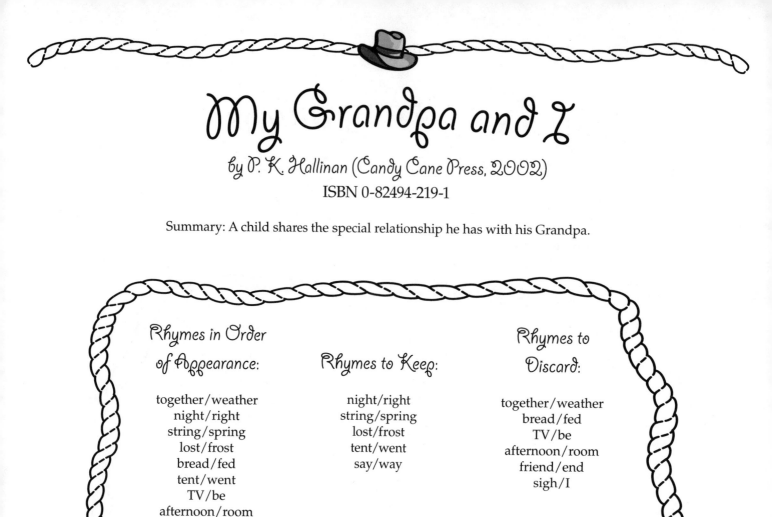

My Grandpa and I

by P. K. Hallinan (Candy Cane Press, 2002)

ISBN 0-82494-219-1

Summary: A child shares the special relationship he has with his Grandpa.

Rhymes in Order of Appearance:

together/weather
night/right
string/spring
lost/frost
bread/fed
tent/went
TV/be
afternoon/room
friend/end
say/way
sigh/I

Rhymes to Keep:

night/right
string/spring
lost/frost
tent/went
say/way

Rhymes to Discard:

together/weather
bread/fed
TV/be
afternoon/room
friend/end
sigh/I

8–10 rhymes is enough to "round up." See pages 7-14 for step-by-step instructions.

My Hippie Grandmother

by Reeve Lindbergh (Candlewick Press, 2003)

ISBN 0-76360-671-5

Summary: A little girl shares what makes her time with her grandmother so special.

Rhymes in Order of Appearance:

mine/nine
Russ/bus
Tim/Jim
shower/power
beans/jeans
Saturday/away
hall/all
guitar/star
feet/sheet
TV/me
space/race
do/you

Rhymes to Keep:

mine/nine
Tim/Jim
shower/power
beans/jeans
Saturday/away
hall/all
guitar/star
feet/sheet
space/race

Rhymes to Discard:

Russ/bus
TV/me
do/you

8–10 rhymes is enough to "round up." See pages 7-14 for step-by-step instructions.

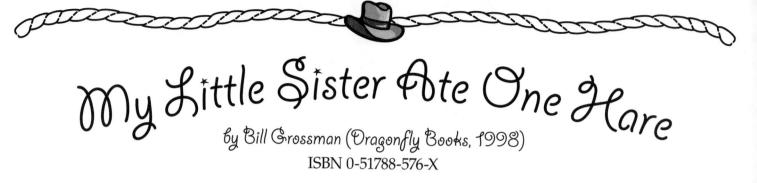

My Little Sister Ate One Hare

by Bill Grossman (Dragonfly Books, 1998)
ISBN 0-51788-576-X

Summary: We thought she would throw up as soon as she ate one hare, but little sister didn't. Read to find out what she eats and what finally causes quite a disturbance.

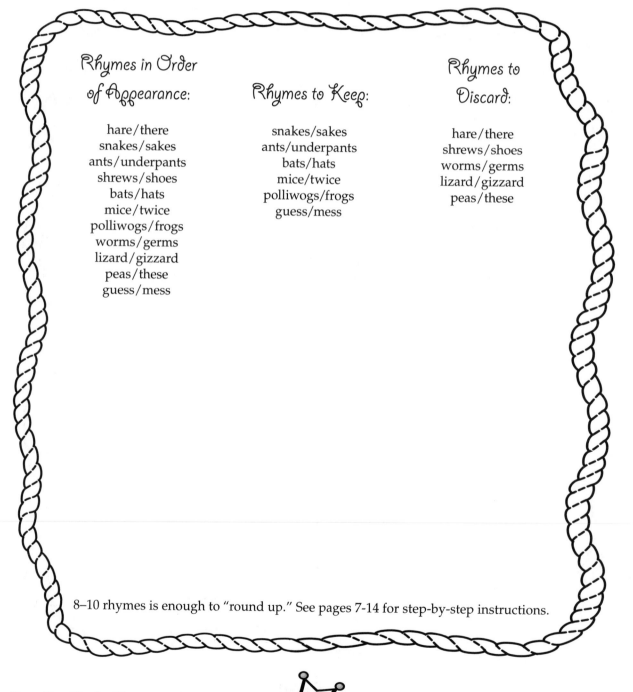

Rhymes in Order of Appearance:

hare/there
snakes/sakes
ants/underpants
shrews/shoes
bats/hats
mice/twice
polliwogs/frogs
worms/germs
lizard/gizzard
peas/these
guess/mess

Rhymes to Keep:

snakes/sakes
ants/underpants
bats/hats
mice/twice
polliwogs/frogs
guess/mess

Rhymes to Discard:

hare/there
shrews/shoes
worms/germs
lizard/gizzard
peas/these

8–10 rhymes is enough to "round up." See pages 7-14 for step-by-step instructions.

Mystery Mansion

by Michael Garland (Puffin Books, 2003)

ISBN 0-14250-084-4

Summary: Join Tommy on a special hunt in his Aunt Jeanne's mansion. Use the letter and picture clues to help him find the surprise.

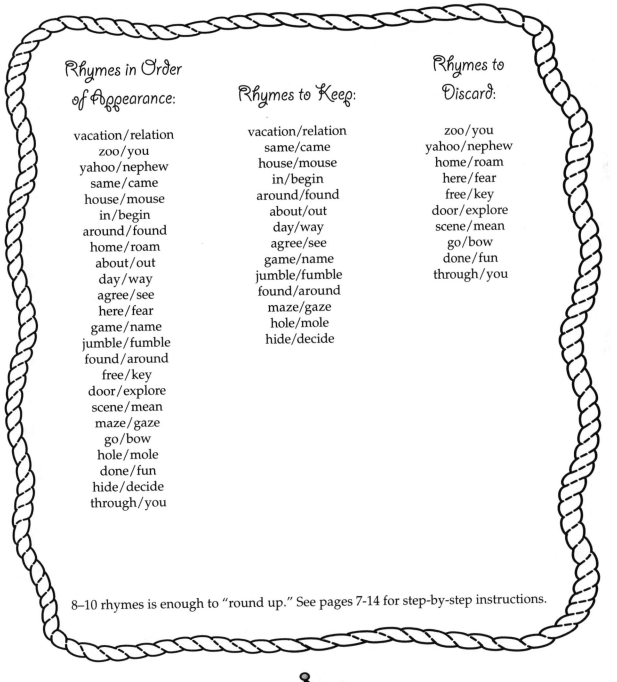

Rhymes in Order of Appearance:

vacation/relation
zoo/you
yahoo/nephew
same/came
house/mouse
in/begin
around/found
home/roam
about/out
day/way
agree/see
here/fear
game/name
jumble/fumble
found/around
free/key
door/explore
scene/mean
maze/gaze
go/bow
hole/mole
done/fun
hide/decide
through/you

Rhymes to Keep:

vacation/relation
same/came
house/mouse
in/begin
around/found
about/out
day/way
agree/see
game/name
jumble/fumble
found/around
maze/gaze
hole/mole
hide/decide

Rhymes to Discard:

zoo/you
yahoo/nephew
home/roam
here/fear
free/key
door/explore
scene/mean
go/bow
done/fun
through/you

8–10 rhymes is enough to "round up." See pages 7-14 for step-by-step instructions.

Rounding Up the Rhymes • Grades 1–3

The Night Before Easter

by Natasha Wing (Grosset and Dunlap, 1999)

ISBN 0-44841-873-8

Summary: The children have set out their baskets in anticipation of the Easter Bunny's visit. The little boy surreptitiously watches as the bunny and his assistant pay a call and fill the baskets with all kinds of goodies.

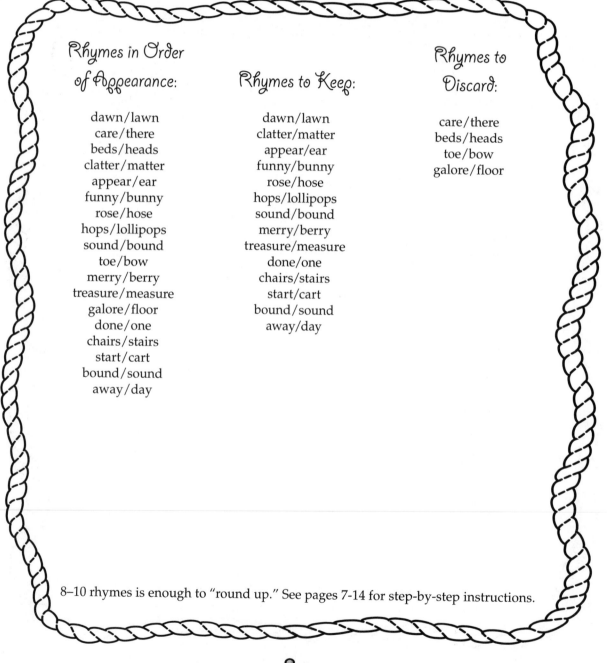

Rhymes in Order of Appearance:

dawn/lawn
care/there
beds/heads
clatter/matter
appear/ear
funny/bunny
rose/hose
hops/lollipops
sound/bound
toe/bow
merry/berry
treasure/measure
galore/floor
done/one
chairs/stairs
start/cart
bound/sound
away/day

Rhymes to Keep:

dawn/lawn
clatter/matter
appear/ear
funny/bunny
rose/hose
hops/lollipops
sound/bound
merry/berry
treasure/measure
done/one
chairs/stairs
start/cart
bound/sound
away/day

Rhymes to Discard:

care/there
beds/heads
toe/bow
galore/floor

8–10 rhymes is enough to "round up." See pages 7-14 for step-by-step instructions.

80

The Night Before Kindergarten

by Natasha Wing (Grosset and Dunlap, 2001)

ISBN 0-44842-500-9

Summary: The children are excited and a little anxious about the first day of school. There are so many unknowns as they eagerly anticipate kindergarten. Parents are a bit worried, as well. Visit with them as they prepare for and experience the first day of kindergarten.

Rhymes in Order of Appearance:

prepared/scared
beds/heads
galore/door
care/there
today/play
white/bright
cars/Mars
bear/care
wow/now
cry/good-bye
stay/A-okay
smile/while
maps/naps
end/friend
Sunrise/surprise
wet/yet
rug/hug
school/cool

Rhymes to Keep:

prepared/scared
today/play
cars/Mars
wow/now
stay/A-okay
smile/while
maps/naps
Sunrise/surprise
wet/yet
rug/hug
school/cool

Rhymes to Discard:

beds/heads
galore/door
care/there
white/bright
bear/care
cry/good-bye
end/friend

8–10 rhymes is enough to "round up." See pages 7-14 for step-by-step instructions.

The Night Before the Night Before Christmas

by Natasha Wing (Grosset and Dunlap, 2002)

ISBN 0-44842-872-5

Summary: Christmas Day is just around the corner and nothing is ready. Mom is sick, and the other family members are trying to get things lined up for the holiday celebration. In the midst of all the confusion, the family discovers the true meaning of Christmas.

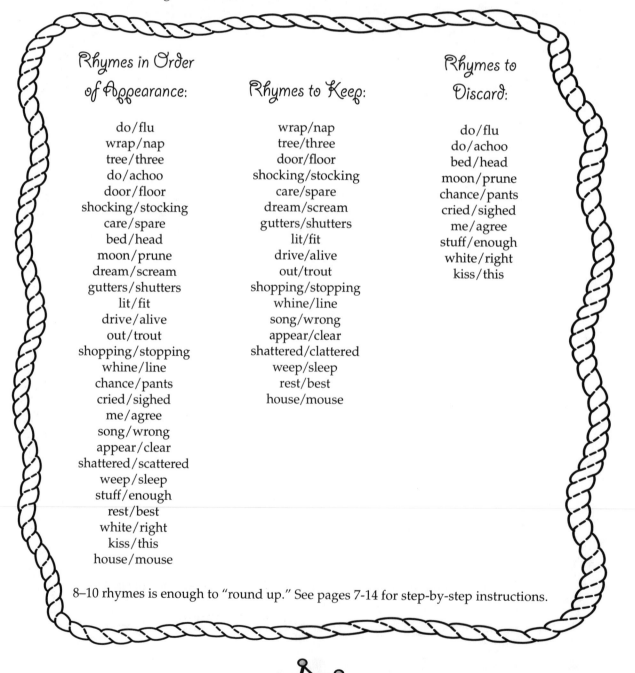

Rhymes in Order of Appearance:

do/flu
wrap/nap
tree/three
do/achoo
door/floor
shocking/stocking
care/spare
bed/head
moon/prune
dream/scream
gutters/shutters
lit/fit
drive/alive
out/trout
shopping/stopping
whine/line
chance/pants
cried/sighed
me/agree
song/wrong
appear/clear
shattered/scattered
weep/sleep
stuff/enough
rest/best
white/right
kiss/this
house/mouse

Rhymes to Keep:

wrap/nap
tree/three
door/floor
shocking/stocking
care/spare
dream/scream
gutters/shutters
lit/fit
drive/alive
out/trout
shopping/stopping
whine/line
song/wrong
appear/clear
shattered/clattered
weep/sleep
rest/best
house/mouse

Rhymes to Discard:

do/flu
do/achoo
bed/head
moon/prune
chance/pants
cried/sighed
me/agree
stuff/enough
white/right
kiss/this

8–10 rhymes is enough to "round up." See pages 7-14 for step-by-step instructions.

The Night Before Summer Vacation

by Natasha Wing (Grosset and Dunlap, 2002)

ISBN 0-448-42830-X

Summary: The family is very excited about their upcoming vacation. Planning and packing create quite a whirlwind. When the family departs, they realize that they have left behind something very important.

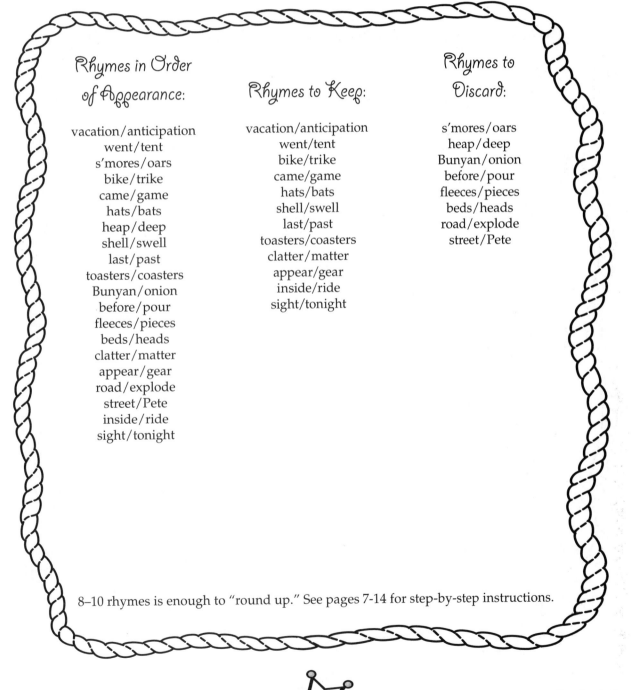

Rhymes in Order of Appearance:

vacation/anticipation
went/tent
s'mores/oars
bike/trike
came/game
hats/bats
heap/deep
shell/swell
last/past
toasters/coasters
Bunyan/onion
before/pour
fleeces/pieces
beds/heads
clatter/matter
appear/gear
road/explode
street/Pete
inside/ride
sight/tonight

Rhymes to Keep:

vacation/anticipation
went/tent
bike/trike
came/game
hats/bats
shell/swell
last/past
toasters/coasters
clatter/matter
appear/gear
inside/ride
sight/tonight

Rhymes to Discard:

s'mores/oars
heap/deep
Bunyan/onion
before/pour
fleeces/pieces
beds/heads
road/explode
street/Pete

8–10 rhymes is enough to "round up." See pages 7-14 for step-by-step instructions.

The Night Before the Tooth Fairy

by Natasha Wing (Grosset and Dunlap, 2003)

ISBN 0-44843-252-8

Summary: A little boy's "loosey" tooth is driving him nuts, but it just won't come out. An altercation between the family's dog and cat causes a commotion, which knocks out the tooth. Now he prepares for the long-awaited visit from the tooth fairy.

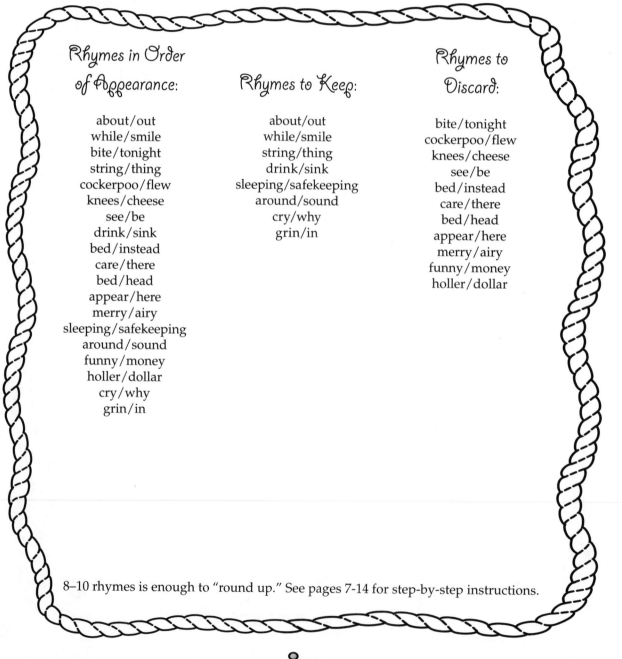

Rhymes in Order of Appearance:

about/out
while/smile
bite/tonight
string/thing
cockerpoo/flew
knees/cheese
see/be
drink/sink
bed/instead
care/there
bed/head
appear/here
merry/airy
sleeping/safekeeping
around/sound
funny/money
holler/dollar
cry/why
grin/in

Rhymes to Keep:

about/out
while/smile
string/thing
drink/sink
sleeping/safekeeping
around/sound
cry/why
grin/in

Rhymes to Discard:

bite/tonight
cockerpoo/flew
knees/cheese
see/be
bed/instead
care/there
bed/head
appear/here
merry/airy
funny/money
holler/dollar

8–10 rhymes is enough to "round up." See pages 7-14 for step-by-step instructions.

The Night Before Valentine's Day

by Natasha Wing (Grosset and Dunlap, 2000)

ISBN 0-44842-188-7

Summary: The children are getting ready for Valentine's Day. They make beautiful valentines to give their friends. Enter their classroom and enjoy the pleasant surprises of this special holiday.

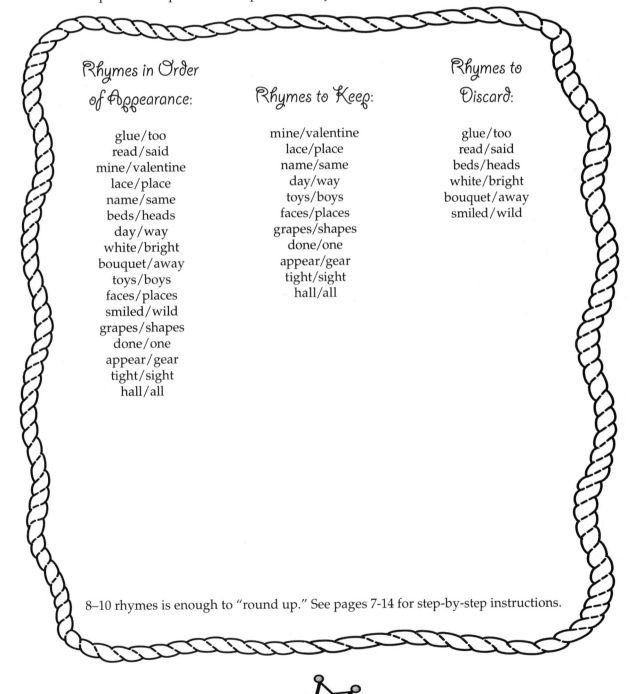

Rhymes in Order of Appearance:

glue/too
read/said
mine/valentine
lace/place
name/same
beds/heads
day/way
white/bright
bouquet/away
toys/boys
faces/places
smiled/wild
grapes/shapes
done/one
appear/gear
tight/sight
hall/all

Rhymes to Keep:

mine/valentine
lace/place
name/same
day/way
toys/boys
faces/places
grapes/shapes
done/one
appear/gear
tight/sight
hall/all

Rhymes to Discard:

glue/too
read/said
beds/heads
white/bright
bouquet/away
smiled/wild

8–10 rhymes is enough to "round up." See pages 7-14 for step-by-step instructions.

Oh, How I Wished I Could Read!

by John Gile (John Gile Communications, 1995)

ISBN 0-91094-110-6

Summary: A little boy suddenly wakes up worried about what he had just experienced in his nightmare. His many misadventures are the results of his inability to read important warning labels and messages in his environment. This is a fun-loving book that has delightful illustrations.

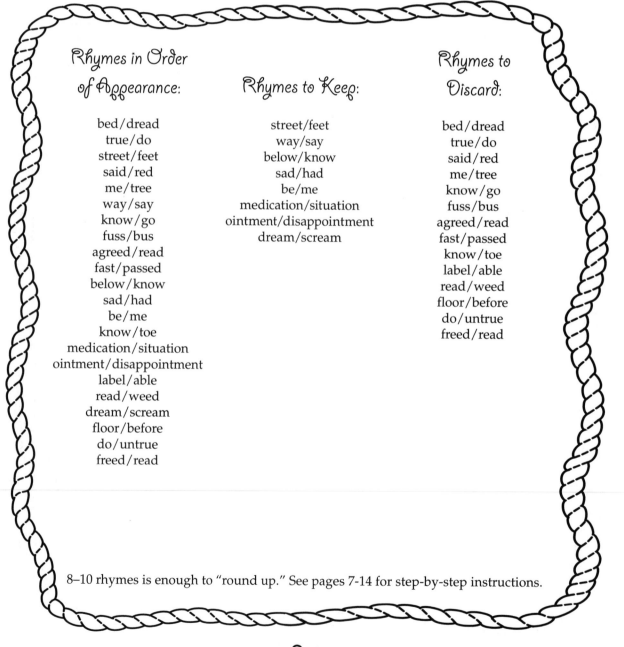

Rhymes in Order of Appearance:

bed/dread
true/do
street/feet
said/red
me/tree
way/say
know/go
fuss/bus
agreed/read
fast/passed
below/know
sad/had
be/me
know/toe
medication/situation
ointment/disappointment
label/able
read/weed
dream/scream
floor/before
do/untrue
freed/read

Rhymes to Keep:

street/feet
way/say
below/know
sad/had
be/me
medication/situation
ointment/disappointment
dream/scream

Rhymes to Discard:

bed/dread
true/do
said/red
me/tree
know/go
fuss/bus
agreed/read
fast/passed
know/toe
label/able
read/weed
floor/before
do/untrue
freed/read

8–10 rhymes is enough to "round up." See pages 7-14 for step-by-step instructions.

Over in the Garden

by Jennifer Ward (Rising Moon Books, 2002)
ISBN 0-87358-793-6

Summary: This is a beautifully illustrated rhyming and counting book. Children are introduced to animals within the garden. Number concepts are supported as children look for the hidden numerals on each page spread. There is a fun fact section at the end of the book that gives information about each of the featured animals.

Rhymes in Order of Appearance:

sun/one
grew/two
tree/three
floor/four
thrive/five
mix/six
heaven/seven
gate/eight
vine/nine
again/ten

Rhymes to Keep:

tree/three
thrive/five
mix/six
vine/nine

Rhymes to Discard:

sun/one
grew/two
floor/four
heaven/seven
gate/eight
again/ten

See pages 7-14 for step-by-step instructions.

87

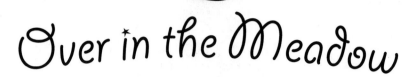

Over in the Meadow

by Olive A. Wadsworth (North-South Books, 2002)

ISBN 0-73581-596-8

Summary: This 19th-century counting rhyme takes place in a meadow. There are a variety of animals for children to count.

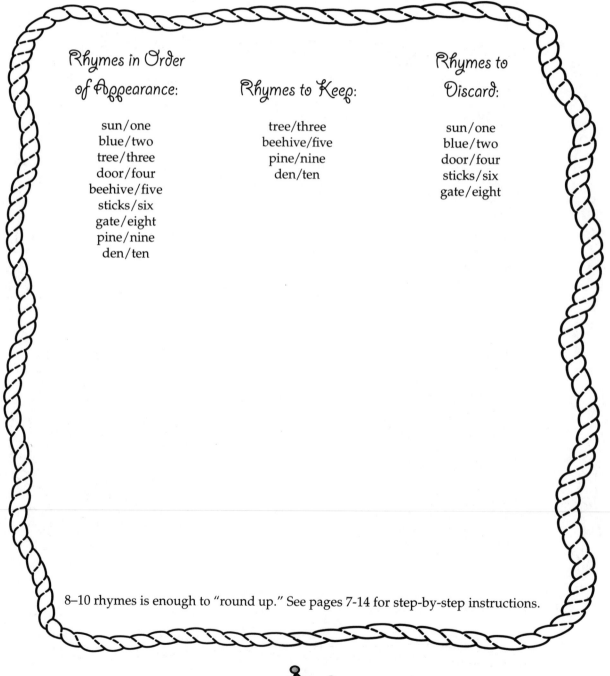

Rhymes in Order of Appearance:

sun/one
blue/two
tree/three
door/four
beehive/five
sticks/six
gate/eight
pine/nine
den/ten

Rhymes to Keep:

tree/three
beehive/five
pine/nine
den/ten

Rhymes to Discard:

sun/one
blue/two
door/four
sticks/six
gate/eight

8–10 rhymes is enough to "round up." See pages 7-14 for step-by-step instructions.

Parts

by Tedd Arnold (Puffin Books, 2000)

ISBN 0-14056-533-7

Summary: A five-year-old boy is worried because his body seems to be falling apart. He finally discusses the situation with his parents and is assured that things are fine. Children are delighted by the "gross factor" and illustrations.

Rhymes in Order of Appearance:

be/me
aware/hair
appalled/bald
was/fuzz
about/out
hose/toes
groan/bone
clothes/nose
pain/brain
Seuss/loose
speak/weak
be/see/me
go/know
off/cough
shape/tape
out/sprout
fear/hear/ear

Rhymes to Keep:

be/me
about/out
pain/brain
speak/weak
shape/tape
out/sprout
fear/hear/ear

Rhymes to Discard:

aware/hair
appalled/bald
was/fuzz
hose/toes
groan/bone
clothes/nose
Seuss/loose
see/me
go/know
off/cough

8–10 rhymes is enough to "round up." See pages 7-14 for step-by-step instructions.

Put Me in the Zoo

by Robert Lopshire (Random House Books for Young Readers, 1960)

ISBN 0-39480-017-6

Summary: A strange-looking, spotted animal attempts to get into the zoo but is not accepted by the zookeepers. The animal meets two children who question why he should be in the zoo. He shows them the amazing things he can do with spots. The children decide that maybe the zoo really isn't the place for him. Perhaps the circus would be a better choice.

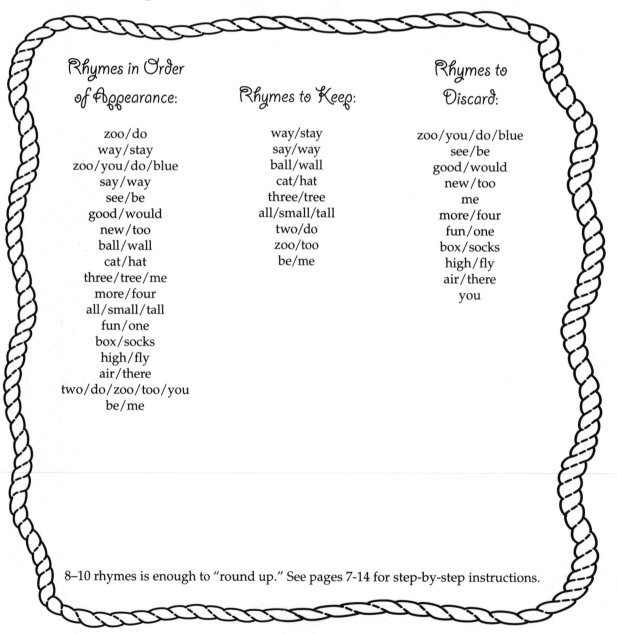

Rhymes in Order of Appearance:	Rhymes to Keep:	Rhymes to Discard:
zoo / do	way / stay	zoo / you / do / blue
way / stay	say / way	see / be
zoo / you / do / blue	ball / wall	good / would
say / way	cat / hat	new / too
see / be	three / tree	me
good / would	all / small / tall	more / four
new / too	two / do	fun / one
ball / wall	zoo / too	box / socks
cat / hat	be / me	high / fly
three / tree / me		air / there
more / four		you
all / small / tall		
fun / one		
box / socks		
high / fly		
air / there		
two / do / zoo / too / you		
be / me		

8–10 rhymes is enough to "round up." See pages 7-14 for step-by-step instructions.

90

Quick as a Cricket

by Audrey Wood (Child's Play International, Ltd., 1990)

ISBN 0-85953-306-9

Summary: A little boy compares himself to many different animals. This book provides great examples of similes. Beautiful illustrations accompany the text.

Rhymes in Order
of Appearance:

snail/whale
lark/shark
fox/ox
clam/lamb
shrimp/chimp
bee/me

Rhymes to Keep:

lark/shark
fox/ox
shrimp/chimp

Rhymes to
Discard:

snail/whale
clam/lamb
bee/me

See pages 7-14 for step-by-step instructions.

Rabbit's Pajama Party

by Stuart J. Murphy (HarperTrophy, 1999)

ISBN 0-06446-722-8

Summary: Teach sequential order with this fun-loving story filled with the many activities Rabbit and his friends enjoy at their pajama party.

Rhymes in Order of Appearance:

begin/in
cheese/please
cream/dream
bed/red
right/tight
laugh/Giraffe
rest/best
roar/snore

Rhymes to Keep:

begin/in
cream/dream
bed/red
right/tight
rest/best

Rhymes to Discard:

cheese/please
laugh/Giraffe
roar/snore

See pages 7-14 for step-by-step instructions.

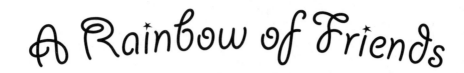

A Rainbow of Friends

by P. K. Hallinan (Ideals Publications, 2002)

ISBN 0-82495-395-9

Summary: An awareness and appreciation is shared in this book of diversity and acceptance.

Rhymes in Order of Appearance:

see/harmony
stars/ours
way/say
share/care
speech/reach
hearts/apart
all/fall
views/too
far/are
together/weather
done/won
meet/greet
depends/friends

Rhymes to Keep:

way/say
share/care
all/fall
meet/greet

Rhymes to Discard:

see/harmony
stars/ours
speech/reach
hearts/apart
views/too
far/are
together/weather
done/won
depends/friends

8–10 rhymes is enough to "round up." See pages 7-14 for step-by-step instructions.

The Rules

by Marty Kelley (Knowledge Unlimited, 2000)
ISBN 1-55933-284-0

Summary: Kids have lots of rules to learn. Some of these rules are examined and enjoyed through the delightful verse and pictures in this book.

Rhymes in Order of Appearance:

hair/underwear
back/snack
hands/bands
dirt/hurt
curse/worse
nose/toes
rude/food
away/way
clothes/nose
shirt/dessert
bed/said
done/fun

Rhymes to Keep:

back/snack
hands/bands
away/way

Rhymes to Discard:

hair/underwear
dirt/hurt
curse/worse
nose/toes
rude/food
clothes/nose
shirt/dessert
bed/said
done/fun

8–10 rhymes is enough to "round up." See pages 7-14 for step-by-step instructions.

Rumble in the Jungle

by Giles Andreae (Tiger Tales, 2001)

ISBN 1-58925-005-2

Summary: This is a delightful, rhyming journey through the jungle. Children will meet many of the animals that live in that environment. Colorful, imaginative illustrations accompany the text.

Rhymes in Order of Appearance:

trees/leaves
lair/everywhere
kind/find
trees/fleas
paws/jaws
quivers/shivers
round/around
mule/cool
prey/way
proud/cloud
care/air
hot/lot
two/few
delight/sight
flappy/happy
gazelle/well
high/sky
hairy/scary
best/chest
night/polite
near/fear
lights/nights
sleeps/creeps
growl/prowl
den/again

Rhymes to Keep:

kind/find
paws/jaws
quivers/shivers
round/around
proud/cloud
hot/lot
delight/sight
flappy/happy
best/chest
near/fear
lights/nights
sleeps/creeps
growl/prowl

Rhymes to Discard:

trees/leaves
lair/everywhere
trees/fleas
mule/cool
prey/way
care/air
two/few
gazelle/well
high/sky
hairy/scary
night/polite
den/again

8–10 rhymes is enough to "round up." See pages 7-14 for step-by-step instructions.

The Shape of Things

by Dayle Ann Dodds (Candlewick Press, 1996)

ISBN 1-56402-698-1

Summary: Illustrations contain the shapes featured in the text. Children can match the shapes and enjoy the embellishments as they learn about circles, squares, diamonds, triangles, rectangles, and ovals.

Rhymes in Order of Appearance:	Rhymes to Keep:	Rhymes to Discard:
door/more	sky/by	door/more
low/go	track/back	low/go
sky/by	then/hen	
track/back	tail/sail	
then/hen	kind/find	
tail/sail		
kind/find		

See pages 7-14 for step-by-step instructions.

Skittles® Riddles Math

by Barbara Barbieri McGrath (Charlesbridge Publishing, 2001)

ISBN 1-57091-413-3

Summary: The math concepts of negative numbers, number lines, quantity comparison, number sentences, and fractions are targeted in this book. Students are entertained with Skittles® and riddles as they contemplate the problems they encounter.

Rhymes in Order of Appearance:

go/rainbow
fun/begun
compare/there
count/amount
sixteen/between
zero/hero
proceed/indeed
sweet/treat
confusing/using
twenty/plenty
see/carefully
name/same
green/seen
goal/whole
done/one

Rhymes to Keep:

fun/begun
count/amount
sixteen/between
zero/hero
proceed/indeed
confusing/using
twenty/plenty
name/same
green/seen
done/one

Rhymes to Discard:

go/rainbow
compare/there
sweet/treat
see/carefully
goal/whole

8–10 rhymes is enough to "round up." See pages 7-14 for step-by-step instructions.

Sleepless Beauty

by Frances Minters (Puffin Books, 1999)

ISBN 0-14056-619-8

Summary: A selection that is a spin-off of Sleeping Beauty in a modern setting with an independent main character named Little Beauty.

Rhymes in Order of Appearance:

tooty/beauty
cutie/beauty
me/3D
town/down
celebration/invitation
nonetheless/dress
kiss/miss
her/finger
fair/care
snooty/beauty
child/wild
planned/hand
pin/skin
why/pie
ice/twice
hair/care
boom/room
witch/hitch
here/dear
round/sound
there/scared
ouch/couch
duty/beauty
cat/mat
said/bed
awoke/joke
say/yesterday
harm/alarm
rock/clock
school/cool
stranger/danger
kazootie/beauty
guess/yes

Rhymes to Keep:

town/down
celebration/invitation
nonetheless/dress
kiss/miss
her/finger
child/wild
pin/skin
ice/twice
boom/room
witch/hitch
round/sound
ouch/couch
deep/sleep
cat/mat
awoke/joke
say/yesterday
harm/alarm
rock/clock
school/cool
stranger/danger

Rhymes to Discard:

tooty/beauty
cutie/beauty
me/3D
fair/care
snooty/beauty
planned/hand
why/pie
hair/care
here/dear
there/scared
duty/beauty
said/bed
kazootie/beauty
guess/yes

8–10 rhymes is enough to "round up." See pages 7-14 for step-by-step instructions.

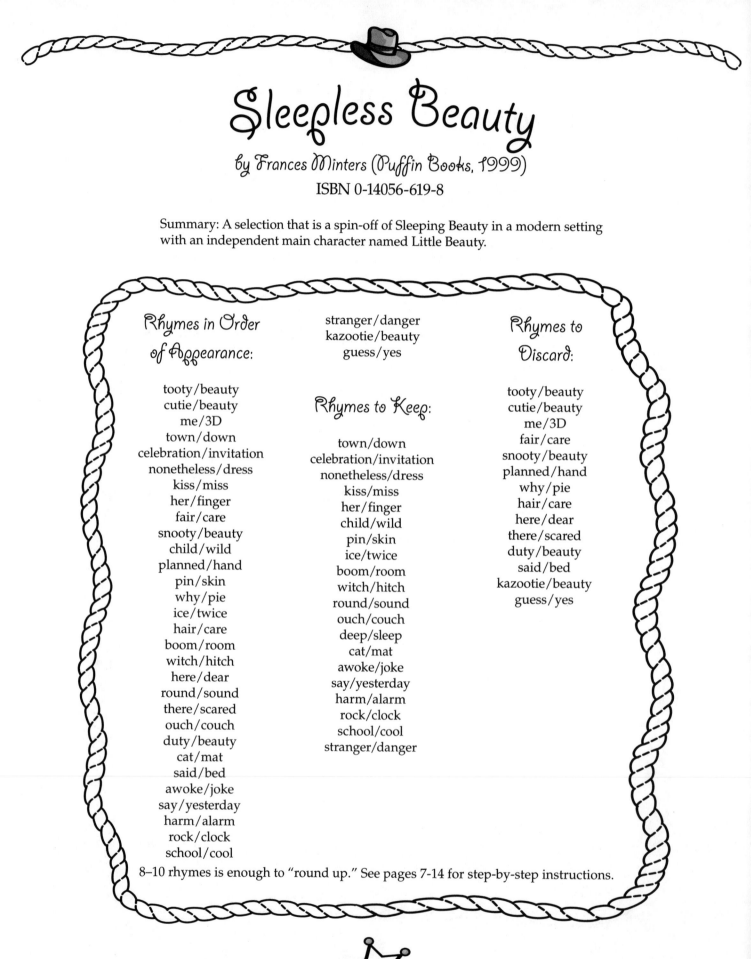

98

Somewhere in the Ocean

by Jennifer Ward and T. J. Marsh (Rising Moon Books, 2000)

ISBN 0-87358-748-0

Summary: This is a beautifully illustrated counting and rhyming book that also introduces concepts about the ocean biome. Children read about sea animals and their habitats. Number recognition is also supported as children search for the hidden numerals on each page. There is an expository section at the end of the book that features facts about each of the animals and certain habitats featured in the text.

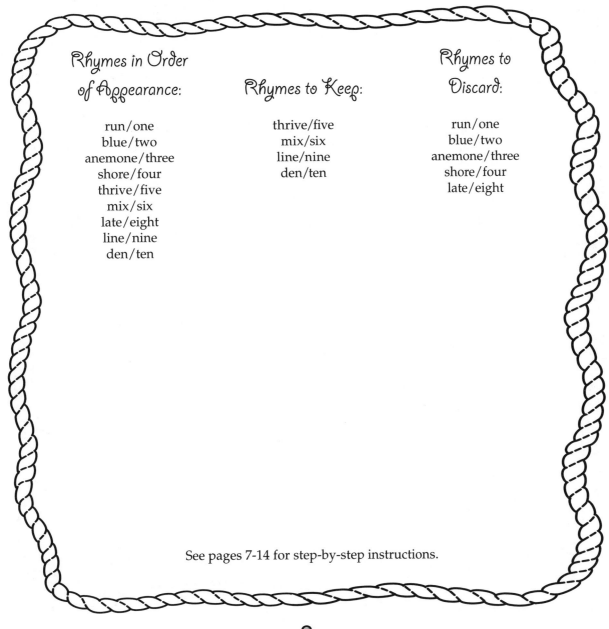

Rhymes in Order of Appearance:

run/one
blue/two
anemone/three
shore/four
thrive/five
mix/six
late/eight
line/nine
den/ten

Rhymes to Keep:

thrive/five
mix/six
line/nine
den/ten

Rhymes to Discard:

run/one
blue/two
anemone/three
shore/four
late/eight

See pages 7-14 for step-by-step instructions.

Summer Stinks

by Marty Kelley (Zino Press Children's Books, 2001)

ISBN 1-55933-291-3

Summary: In this alphabet book, a boy shares 26 different reasons why summer should be avoided.

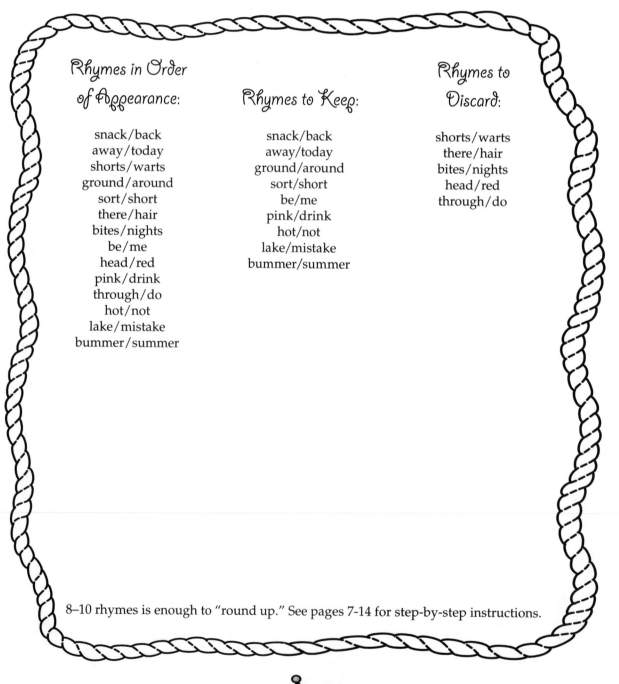

Rhymes in Order of Appearance:

snack/back
away/today
shorts/warts
ground/around
sort/short
there/hair
bites/nights
be/me
head/red
pink/drink
through/do
hot/not
lake/mistake
bummer/summer

Rhymes to Keep:

snack/back
away/today
ground/around
sort/short
be/me
pink/drink
hot/not
lake/mistake
bummer/summer

Rhymes to Discard:

shorts/warts
there/hair
bites/nights
head/red
through/do

8–10 rhymes is enough to "round up." See pages 7-14 for step-by-step instructions.

The Thingumajig Book of Manners

by Irene Keller (Ideals Children's Books, 2001)

ISBN 0-82495-434-3

Summary: The Thingumajigs have terrible manners. Their awful habits are contrasted with the manners that we should have.

Rhymes in Order of Appearance:

snails/fingernails
see/me
pigs/Thingumajigs
should/good
fight/night
fair/everywhere
spit/bit
icky/sticky
please/sneeze
others/brothers/mothers
grunts/once
please/these
which/itch
bite/fight/Night
found/round
boys/toys
grow/know
say/play
same/game
chores/doors
share/fair
look/Book

Rhymes to Keep:

snails/fingernails
pigs/Thingumajigs
fight/night
spit/bit
icky/sticky
others/brothers/mothers
fight/Night
found/round
boys/toys
grow/know
say/play
same/game
look/Book

Rhymes to Discard:

see/me
should/good
fair/everywhere
please/sneeze
grunts/once
please/these
which/itch
bite
chores/doors
share/fair

8–10 rhymes is enough to "round up." See pages 7-14 for step-by-step instructions.

This Is the Sea that Feeds Us

by Robert F. Baldwin (Dawn Publications, 1998)

ISBN 1-88322-070-X

Summary: This book explores the ocean's fabulous food chain. A new link is introduced in each verse. Repeated rhymes and inspiring illustrations lend to the charm of this delightful book. Expository text that accompanies each rhyming page spread is wonderful support for science content.

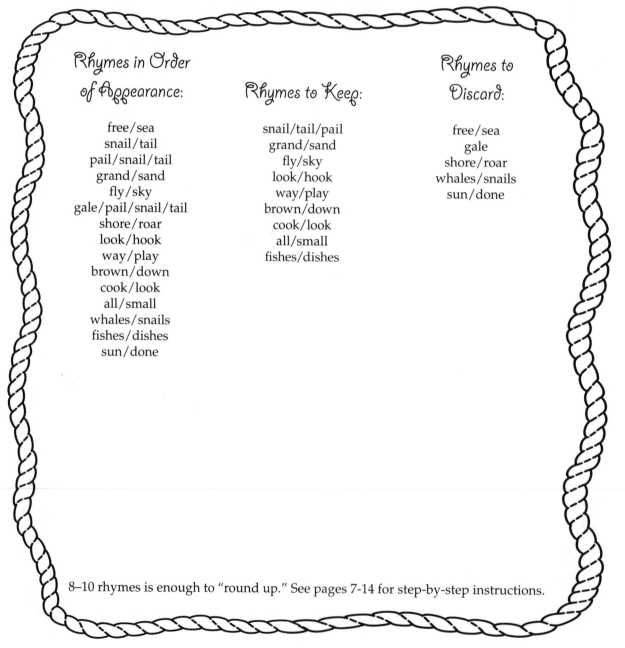

Rhymes in Order of Appearance:	Rhymes to Keep:	Rhymes to Discard:
free/sea	snail/tail/pail	free/sea
snail/tail	grand/sand	gale
pail/snail/tail	fly/sky	shore/roar
grand/sand	look/hook	whales/snails
fly/sky	way/play	sun/done
gale/pail/snail/tail	brown/down	
shore/roar	cook/look	
look/hook	all/small	
way/play	fishes/dishes	
brown/down		
cook/look		
all/small		
whales/snails		
fishes/dishes		
sun/done		

8–10 rhymes is enough to "round up." See pages 7-14 for step-by-step instructions.

This Is the Way We Go to School

by Edith Baer (Scholastic, 1992)

ISBN 0-59043-162-5

Summary: Discover how students across the world travel to school. Integrate geography and transportation with this informative selection.

Rhymes in Order of Appearance:

two/do
slow/grow
rule/school
past/fast
far/car
Perry/Ferry
Jill/hill
Miguel/El
plain/Jane
Molly/trolley
Benedetto/vaporetto
breeze/skis
cool/school
play/away
sail/vale
train/chain
Joe/radio
Ling/Nanjing
sky/dry
boat/afloat
stride/countryside
line/fine
Skidoo/do/you

Rhymes to Keep:

slow/grow
past/fast
far/car
Perry/Ferry
Jill/hill
Benedetto/vaporetto
cool/school
play/away
train/chain
Ling/Nanjing
sky/dry
boat/afloat
stride/countryside
line/fine

Rhymes to Discard:

two/do
rule/school
Miguel/El
plain/Jane
Molly/trolley
breeze/skis
sail/vale
Joe/radio
Skidoo/do/you

8–10 rhymes is enough to "round up." See pages 7-14 for step-by-step instructions.

Today Is Thanksgiving

by P. K. Hallinan (Ideals Publications, 2001)

ISBN 0-82495-326-6

Summary: Share in the festive activities as a family prepares for a full day of Thanksgiving memory-making.

Rhymes in Order of Appearance:

breeze/leaves
haze/maize
tow/go
swell/well
air/hair
guessing/dressing
in/thin
done/sun
tweeks/cheeks
goals/poles
kick/click
pass/grass
clan/Stan
bearing/sharing
nieces/sneezes
chair/hair
resounds/sounds
begin/grin
ahs/applause
prayer/there
dream/cream
sigh/pie
fun/everyone
say/day

Rhymes to Keep:

swell/well
air/hair
guessing/dressing
in/thin
tweeks/cheeks
kick/click
pass/grass
clan/Stan
chair/hair
resounds/sounds
begin/grin
dream/cream
say/day

Rhymes to Discard:

breeze/leaves
haze/maize
tow/go
done/sun
goals/poles
bearing/sharing
nieces/sneezes
ahs/applause
prayer/there
sigh/pie
fun/everyone

8–10 rhymes is enough to "round up." See pages 7-14 for step-by-step instructions.

'Twas the Day AFTER Thanksgiving

by Mavis Smith (Little Simon, 2002)

ISBN 0-68985-234-7

Summary: The mouse family enjoys leftovers after the Thanksgiving feast. Interesting surprises await under the page flaps as we journey through the day.

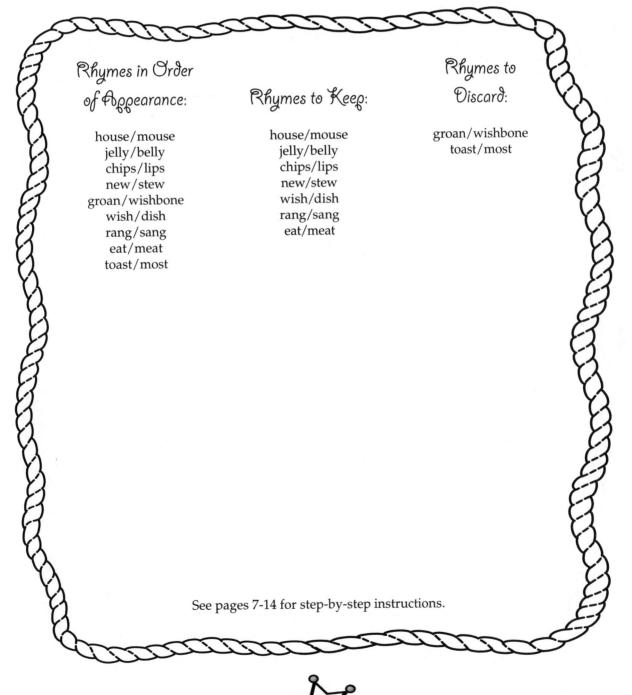

Rhymes in Order of Appearance:

house/mouse
jelly/belly
chips/lips
new/stew
groan/wishbone
wish/dish
rang/sang
eat/meat
toast/most

Rhymes to Keep:

house/mouse
jelly/belly
chips/lips
new/stew
wish/dish
rang/sang
eat/meat

Rhymes to Discard:

groan/wishbone
toast/most

See pages 7-14 for step-by-step instructions.

Rounding Up the Rhymes • Grades 1–3

'Twas the Night Before Thanksgiving

by Dav Pilkey (Scholastic, 2004)

ISBN 0-43966-937-5

Summary: The class is taking a field trip to a turkey farm on the day before Thanksgiving. The children are horrified at the fate awaiting these turkeys. With a little ingenuity by the students, there is a happy ending for everyone, including the turkeys.

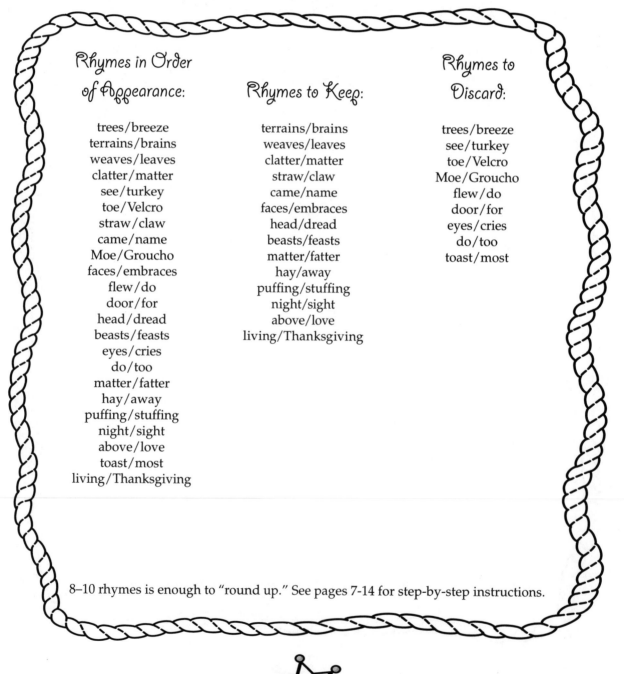

Rhymes in Order of Appearance:	Rhymes to Keep:	Rhymes to Discard:
trees/breeze	terrains/brains	trees/breeze
terrains/brains	weaves/leaves	see/turkey
weaves/leaves	clatter/matter	toe/Velcro
clatter/matter	straw/claw	Moe/Groucho
see/turkey	came/name	flew/do
toe/Velcro	faces/embraces	door/for
straw/claw	head/dread	eyes/cries
came/name	beasts/feasts	do/too
Moe/Groucho	matter/fatter	toast/most
faces/embraces	hay/away	
flew/do	puffing/stuffing	
door/for	night/sight	
head/dread	above/love	
beasts/feasts	living/Thanksgiving	
eyes/cries		
do/too		
matter/fatter		
hay/away		
puffing/stuffing		
night/sight		
above/love		
toast/most		
living/Thanksgiving		

8–10 rhymes is enough to "round up." See pages 7-14 for step-by-step instructions.

The Way I Feel

by Janan Cain (Parenting Press, 2000)
ISBN 1-88473-471-5

Summary: This book helps children learn the language to express how they are feeling. A variety of emotions is explored as we visit with our little friend who is experiencing a gamut of feelings.

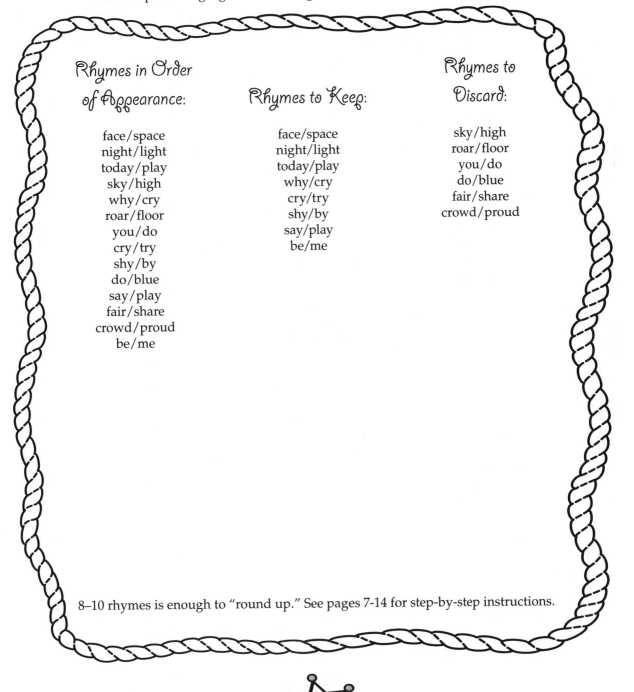

Rhymes in Order of Appearance:

face/space
night/light
today/play
sky/high
why/cry
roar/floor
you/do
cry/try
shy/by
do/blue
say/play
fair/share
crowd/proud
be/me

Rhymes to Keep:

face/space
night/light
today/play
why/cry
cry/try
shy/by
say/play
be/me

Rhymes to Discard:

sky/high
roar/floor
you/do
do/blue
fair/share
crowd/proud

8–10 rhymes is enough to "round up." See pages 7-14 for step-by-step instructions.

Rounding Up the Rhymes • Grades 1–3

The Wedding

by Eve Bunting (Charlesbridge Publishing, 2003)
ISBN 1-58089-040-7

Summary: As Miss Brindle Cow is walking along she meets many creatures that are having difficulty getting to a wedding on time. Being a kind-hearted cow, she offers to help and ends up surprising her new friends as they arrive at the church.

Rhymes in Order of Appearance:

brown/town
tree/knee
church/lurch (no transfer words)
good/could
despair/there
down/town
slow/ago
Pomeroy/joy
say/today
gloomy/roomy
feet/eat
me/catastrophe
there/prayer
down/town
gate/late
city/pretty
blusher/usher (no transfer words)
date/late
needed/proceeded
knew/do
affair/where
exhausted/frosted
hash/mash
food/multitude
shy/high
overhead/said
along/song
nice/twice

you/do
stop/top
Me/tenderly
starry-eyed/bride
here/dear
you/new
strong/along
inside/bride

Rhymes to Keep:

brown/town
tree/knee
down/town
Pomeroy/joy
say/today
gloomy/roomy
me/catastrophe
down/town
gate/late
date/late
needed/proceeded
hash/mash
along/song
nice/twice
stop/top
strong/along
inside/bride

Rhymes to Discard:

church/lurch (no transfer words)
good/could
despair/there
slow/ago
feet/eat
there/prayer
city/pretty
blusher/usher (no transfer words)
knew/do
affair/where
exhausted/frosted
food/multitude
shy/high
overhead/said
you/do
Me/tenderly
starry-eyed/bride
here/dear
you/new

8–10 rhymes is enough to "round up." See pages 7-14 for step-by-step instructions.

Where Once There Was a Wood

by Denise Fleming (Henry Holt and Co., 2000)

ISBN 0-80506-482-6

Summary: Wildlife areas are becoming limited as homes for creatures compete with human habitats. Information is presented to help children learn how to help create new homes for wild creatures.

Rhymes in Order of Appearance:

grew/dew
brood/food
sight/night
feed/seed

Rhymes to Keep:

grew/dew
brood/food
sight/night
feed/seed

Rhymes to Discard:

8–10 rhymes is enough to "round up." See pages 7-14 for step-by-step instructions.

Wild About Books

by Judy Sierra (Knopf Books for Young Readers, 2004)
ISBN 0-375-82538-X

Summary: The librarian has gone into the zoo by accident. She introduces the animals to reading and helps each animal find the perfect book.

Rhymes in Order of Appearance:

2002/McGrew/zoo
stair/chair
distance/resistance
Seuss/moose
Lynx/skinks
Stampeding/reading
nooks/books
fat/Cat/Hat
new/true/how-to
tall/small/wall
Chinese/please
otter/Potter
bunches/lunches
Drew/zoo/overdue
right/tight
exciting/writing
new/too
bills/quills
zoo/haiku/review
shape/ape
well/tell
surprise/Prize
do/gnu/zoo
ourselves/shelves
day/hooray
mind/find

Rhymes to Keep:

stair/chair
distance/resistance
nooks/books
fat/Cat/Hat
tall/small/wall
otter/Potter
bunches/lunches
right/tight
exciting/writing
bills/quills
shape/ape
well/tell
ourselves/shelves
day/hooray
mind/find

Rhymes to Discard:

2002/McGrew/zoo
Seuss/moose
Lynx/skinks
Stampeding/reading
new/true/how-to
Chinese/please
Drew/zoo/overdue
new/too
zoo/haiku/review
surprise/Prize
do/gnu/zoo

8–10 rhymes is enough to "round up." See pages 7-14 for step-by-step instructions.

110

The Wolf's Story

by Brenda Parkes (Rigby, 2000)

ISBN 0-76356-795-7

Summary: Wolf tells his story about the houses that the pigs built. He explains how he really is not guilty but was just trying to be helpful. Witnesses chime in with corroboration of his story.

Rhymes in Order of Appearance:	Rhymes to Keep:	Rhymes to Discard:
wood/good	wood/good	true/you
true/you	saw/straw	agree/me
agree/me	day/way	wood/should
wood/should	tricks/sticks	enough/puff
saw/straw	all/fall	scene/mean
enough/puff	lie/die	door/more
scene/mean	sticks/bricks	testify/pie
day/way	huffed/puffed	higher/fire
tricks/sticks	strong/wrong	more/door
door/more	out/shout	
all/fall	pot/hot	
lie/die	day/away	
sticks/bricks		
huffed/puffed		
strong/wrong		
testify/pie		
out/shout		
higher/fire		
pot/hot		
more/door		
day/away		

8–10 rhymes is enough to "round up." See pages 7-14 for step-by-step instructions.

Woodrow, the White House Mouse

by Peter W. and Cheryl Shaw Barnes (Scholastic, 2000)

ISBN 0-43912-952-4

Summary: This delightful book tells us about some of the many job responsibilities of the President of the Unites States. It also takes us on a tour of some of the famous locations within the White House.

Rhymes in Order of Appearance:

do/too
house/mouse
vote/wrote
please/cheese
respect/protect
wave/brave
wall/Ball
Bess/less
sons/ones
Art/apart
cheer/chandelier
whoop/soup
agree/see
shelf/himself
busy/dizzy
nation/population
bill/Hill
approved/removed
charge/large
Transportation/Education
Means/Marines
Cheese/agrees
Greets/meets
State/great
play/day
too/blue
fun/everyone
events/gents
day/ballet
Quartet/pirouette
side/hide
seeking/peeking
ceiling/squealing
here/dear
reflection/re-election

Rhymes to Keep:

house/mouse
vote/wrote
respect/protect
wave/brave
wall/Ball
Bess/less
Art/apart
agree/see
shelf/himself
nation/population
bill/Hill
approved/removed
charge/large
Transportation/Education
Greets/meets
play/day
events/gents
side/hide
seeking/peeking
reflection/re-election

Rhymes to Discard:

do/too
please/cheese
sons/ones
cheer/chandelier
whoop/soup
busy/dizzy
Means/Marines
Cheese/agrees
State/great
too/blue
fun/everyone
day/ballet
Quartet/pirouette
ceiling/squealing
here/dear

8–10 rhymes is enough to "round up." See pages 7-14 for step-by-step instructions.

Worry Wart Wes

by Tolya L. Thompson (Savor Publishing, 2002)
ISBN 0-97082-961-2

Summary: Worry Wart Wes stresses about everything! Throughout the book, Wes will share a few of his concerns and how he learns to use different techniques to overcome them.

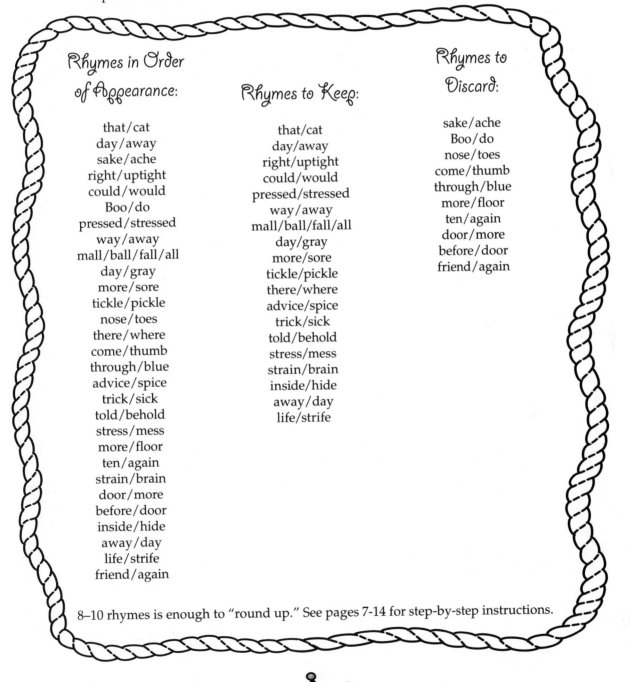

Rhymes in Order of Appearance:

that/cat
day/away
sake/ache
right/uptight
could/would
Boo/do
pressed/stressed
way/away
mall/ball/fall/all
day/gray
more/sore
tickle/pickle
nose/toes
there/where
come/thumb
through/blue
advice/spice
trick/sick
told/behold
stress/mess
more/floor
ten/again
strain/brain
door/more
before/door
inside/hide
away/day
life/strife
friend/again

Rhymes to Keep:

that/cat
day/away
right/uptight
could/would
pressed/stressed
way/away
mall/ball/fall/all
day/gray
more/sore
tickle/pickle
there/where
advice/spice
trick/sick
told/behold
stress/mess
strain/brain
inside/hide
away/day
life/strife

Rhymes to Discard:

sake/ache
Boo/do
nose/toes
come/thumb
through/blue
more/floor
ten/again
door/more
before/door
friend/again

8–10 rhymes is enough to "round up." See pages 7-14 for step-by-step instructions.

113

Yikes—Lice!

by Donna Caffey (Albert Whitman and Co., 2002)

ISBN 0-80759-375-3

Summary: The subject of lice is discussed in this fun-loving rhyming book, with facts included about these pesky critters.

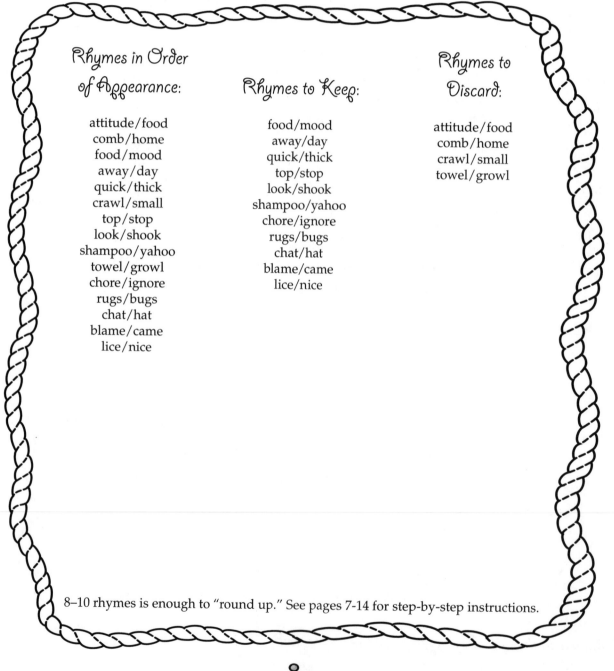

Rhymes in Order of Appearance:

attitude/food
comb/home
food/mood
away/day
quick/thick
crawl/small
top/stop
look/shook
shampoo/yahoo
towel/growl
chore/ignore
rugs/bugs
chat/hat
blame/came
lice/nice

Rhymes to Keep:

food/mood
away/day
quick/thick
top/stop
look/shook
shampoo/yahoo
chore/ignore
rugs/bugs
chat/hat
blame/came
lice/nice

Rhymes to Discard:

attitude/food
comb/home
crawl/small
towel/growl

8–10 rhymes is enough to "round up." See pages 7-14 for step-by-step instructions.

Books by Curriculum Area

General

Bear Wants More by Karma Wilson (Margaret K. McElderry Books, 2003)

Each Peach Pear Plum by Janet and Allan Ahlberg (Puffin Books, 1986)

The Flea's Sneeze by Lynn Downey (Henry Holt and Co., 2000)

Follow Me! by Bethany Roberts (Clarion Books, 1998)

Goodnight Moon by Margaret Wise Brown (HarperTrophy, 1977)

Green Wilma by Tedd Arnold (Puffin Books, 1998)

The Grumpy Morning by Pamela Duncan Edwards (Hyperion, 1998)

Hello School! A Classroom Full of Poems by Dee Lillegard (Dragonfly Books, 2003)

If the Shoe Fits by Alison Jackson (Henry Holt and Co., 2001)

I'll Teach My Dog 100 Words by Michael Frith (HarperCollins Publishers, 1983)

Miss Spider's New Car by David Kirk (Scholastic, 1997)

Mystery Mansion by Michael Garland (Puffin Books, 2003)

The Night Before Kindergarten by Natasha Wing (Grosset and Dunlap, 2001)

Oh, How I Wished I Could Read! by John Gile (John Gile Communications, 1995)

Parts by Tedd Arnold (Puffin Books, 2000)

Put Me in the Zoo by Robert Lopshire (Random House Books for Young Readers, 1960)

The Wedding by Eve Bunting (Charlesbridge Publishing, 2003)

Science

Birds Build Nests by Yvonne Winer (Charlesbridge Publishing, 2002)

Butterflies Fly by Yvonne Winer (Charlesbridge Publishing, 2001)

Don't Call Me Pig!: A Javelina Story by Conrad J. Storad (RGU Group, 1999)

Follow Me! by Bethany Roberts (Clarion Books, 1998)

If I Ran the Rain Forest by Bonnie Worth (Random House Books for Young Readers, 2003)

Lizards for Lunch: A Roadrunner's Tale by Conrad J. Storad (RGU Group, 2002)

Over in the Garden by Jennifer Ward (Rising Moon Books, 2002)

Over in the Meadow: A Counting Rhyme by Olive A. Wadsworth (North-South Books, 2002)

Rumble in the Jungle by Giles Andreae (Tiger Tales, 2001)

Books by Curriculum Area

Somewhere in the Ocean by Jennifer Ward and T. J. Marsh (Rising Moon Books, 2000)

This Is the Sea that Feeds Us by Robert F. Baldwin (Dawn Publications, 1998)

Where Once There Was a Wood by Denise Fleming (Henry Holt and Co., 2000)

Social Studies

House Mouse, Senate Mouse by Peter W. and Cheryl Shaw Barnes (Rosebud Books, 1996)

In 1492 by Jean Marzollo (Scholastic, 1993)

Marshall, the Courthouse Mouse: A Tail of the U.S. Supreme Court by Peter W. and Cheryl Shaw Barnes (Rosebud Books, 1998)

This Is the Way We Go to School by Edith Baer (Scholastic, 1992)

Woodrow, the White House Mouse by Peter W. and Cheryl Shaw Barnes (Scholastic, 2000)

Math

Counting Is for the Birds by Frank Mazzola, Jr. (Charlesbridge Publishing, 1997)

Get Up and Go! by Stuart J. Murphy (HarperTrophy, 1996)

How Many, How Many, How Many by Rick Walton (Candlewick Press, 1996)

Inchworm and a Half by Elinor J. Pinczes (Houghton Mifflin, 2003)

The M&M's® Brand Color Pattern Book by Barbara Barbieri McGrath (Charlesbridge Publishing, 2002)

The M&M's® Brand Counting Book by Barbara Barbieri McGrath (Charlesbridge Publishing, 1994)

More M&M's® Brand Math by Barbara Barbieri McGrath (Charlesbridge Publishing, 1998)

Mr. Monopoly's Amusement Park: A Math Adventure by Jackie Glassman (Scholastic, 2001)

My Little Sister Ate One Hare by Bill Grossman (Dragonfly Books, 1998)

Over in the Garden by Jennifer Ward (Rising Moon Books, 2002)

Over in the Meadow: A Counting Rhyme by Olive A. Wadsworth (North-South Books, 2002)

Rabbit's Pajama Party by Stuart J. Murphy (HarperTrophy, 1999)

The Shape of Things by Dayle Ann Dodds (Candlewick Press, 1996)

Skittles® Riddles Math by Barbara Barbieri McGrath (Charlesbridge Publishing, 2001)

Health

Belly Button Boy by Peter Maloney and Felicia Zekauskas (Puffin Books, 2003)

Books by Curriculum Area

Itchy, Itchy Chicken Pox by Grace MacCarone (Scholastic, 1992)

Loud Lips Lucy by Tolya L. Thompson (Savor Publishing House, 2001)

The Night Before the Tooth Fairy by Natasha Wing (Grosset and Dunlap, 2003)

Worry Wart Wes by Tolya L. Thompson (Savor Publishing, 2002)

Yikes—Lice! by Donna Caffey (Albert Whitman and Co., 2002)

Language Arts

The Bear Came Over to My House by Rick Walton (Puffin Books, 2003)
    question/statement, verb tenses

I Love Words by Barbara Barbieri McGrath (Charlesbridge Publishing, 2003)
    alphabet, vowels, contractions, compound words

The Library by Sarah Stewart (Farrar, Straus and Giroux, 1999)
    love of books, love of reading

Many Luscious Lollipops: A Book about Adjectives by Ruth Heller (Putnam Publishing Group, 1998)
    adjectives

A Mink, a Fink, a Skating Rink: What Is a Noun? by Brian P. Cleary (Carolrhoda Books, Inc., 1999)
    nouns

More Parts by Tedd Arnold (Puffin Books, 2003)
    idioms

Mr. Wiggle's Book by Paula Craig (Instructional Fair, 2001)
    book care

Quick as a Cricket by Audrey Wood (Child's Play International, Ltd., 1990)
    similes

Sleepless Beauty by Frances Minters (Puffin Books, 1999)
    compare/contrast

Wild About Books by Judy Sierra (Knopf Books for Young Readers, 2004)
    reading

The Wolf's Story by Brenda Parkes (Rigby, 2000)
    point of view

Character Education/Life Skills

The Brand New Kid by Katie Couric (Doubleday, 2000)

The Crayon Box that Talked by Shane DeRolf (Random House Books for Young Readers, 1997)

Books by Curriculum Area

Giraffes Can't Dance by Giles Andreae (Scholastic, 2001)

Hooray for You!: A Celebration of You-ness by Marianne Richmond (Marianne Richmond Studios, Inc., 2001)

A Rainbow of Friends by P. K. Hallinan (Ideals Publications, 2002)

The Rules by Marty Kelley (Knowledge Unlimited, 2000)

The Thingumajig Book of Manners by Irene Keller (Ideals Children's Books, 2001)

The Way I Feel by Janan Cain (Parenting Press, 2000)

Seasonal/Holiday

Christmas

Angel Pig and the Hidden Christmas by Jan L. Waldron (Puffin Books, 2000)

The Mouse Before Christmas by Michael Garland (Puffin Books, 2001)

The Night Before the Night Before Christmas by Natasha Wing (Grosset and Dunlap, 2002)

Thanksgiving

Today Is Thanksgiving by P. K. Hallinan (Ideals Publications, 2001)

'Twas the Day AFTER Thanksgiving by Mavis Smith (Little Simon, 2002)

'Twas the Night Before Thanksgiving by Dav Pilkey (Scholastic, 2004)

Mother's Day

I Love You Because You're You by Liza Baker (Cartwheel Books, 2001)

I Love You, Mom by Iris Hiskey Arno (Troll Communications, 2000)

Little Miss Spider by David Kirk (Scholastic Press, 2003)

Motherlove by Virginia Kroll (Dawn Publications, 1998)

Father's Day

The 10 Best Things About My Dad by Christine Loomis (Scholastic Paperbacks, 2004)

My Daddy and I by P. K. Hallinan (Candy Cane Press, 2002)

Books by Curriculum Area

Grandparents Day

My Grandpa and I by P. K. Hallinan (Candy Cane Press, 2002)

My Hippie Grandmother by Reeve Lindbergh (Candlewick Press, 2003)

Valentine's Day

Jennifer Jones Won't Leave Me Alone by Frieda Wishinsky (HarperCollins, 1997)

The Night Before Valentine's Day by Natasha Wing (Grosset and Dunlap, 2000)

Summer

The Best Vacation Ever by Stuart J. Murphy (HarperTrophy, 1997)

How I Spent My Summer Vacation by Mark Teague (Dragonfly Books, 1997)

The Night Before Summer Vacation by Natasha Wing (Grosset and Dunlap, 2002)

Summer Stinks by Marty Kelley (Zino Press Children's Books, 2001)

Easter

The Night Before Easter by Natasha Wing (Grosset and Dunlap, 1999)

St. Patrick's Day

It's St. Patrick's Day! by Rebecca Gomez (Cartwheel Books, 2004)

Spelling Patterns Matched to Books

Word Family	Book(s)	Lesson Page
-able	*Marshall, the Courthouse Mouse*	65
-ace(s*)	*The Brand New Kid*	29
	Hooray for You!	43
	*If the Shoe Fits**	51
	Many Luscious Lollipops	64
	Motherlove	71
	The Mouse Before Christmas	72
	My Hippie Grandmother	77
	*The Night Before Valentine's Day**	85
	*'Twas the Night Before Thanksgiving**	106
	The Way I Feel	107
-ack	*Bear Wants More*	25
	Don't Call Me Pig!	33
	The Grumpy Morning	41
	House Mouse, Senate Mouse	44
	Little Miss Spider	59
	Lizards for Lunch	60
	Mr. Monopoly's Amusement Park	73
	The Rules	94
	The Shape of Things	96
	Summer Stinks	100
-act	*Jennifer Jones Won't Leave Me Alone*	57

* indicates ending appears in the book

Spelling Patterns Matched to Books

Word Family	Book(s)	Lesson Page
-ad	*Giraffes Can't Dance*	38
	Hooray for You!	43
	The Library	58
	Oh, How I Wished I Could Read!	86
-ade	*Birds Build Nests*	28
-ag	*The Mouse Before Christmas*	72
-age	*The Library*	58
-aggler(s*)	*Motherlove**	71
-ail(s*)	*Don't Call Me Pig!*	33
	House Mouse, Senate Mouse	44
	*Many Luscious Lollipops**	64
	A Mink, a Fink, a Skating Rink	67
	The Shape of Things	96
	*The Thingumajig Book of Manners**	101
	This Is the Sea that Feeds Us	102
-ain(s*)	*In 1492*	53
	A Mink, a Fink, a Skating Rink	67
	Motherlove	71
	Parts	89
	This Is the Way We Go to School	103
	*'Twas the Night Before Thanksgiving**	106
	Worry Wart Wes	113
-air(s*)	*Angel Pig and the Hidden Christmas*	23
	I Love You, Mom	49
	*The Night Before Easter**	80

* indicates ending appears in the book

Rounding Up the Rhymes • Grades 1–3

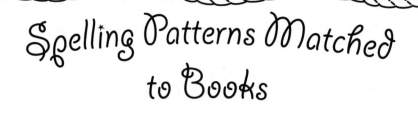

Spelling Patterns Matched to Books

Word Family	Book(s)	Lesson Page
-air(s*) (cont'd)	*Today Is Thanksgiving*	104
	Wild About Books	110
-ake(s*)	*The Bear Came Over to My House*	24
	Get Up and Go!	37
	Hello School!	42
	I Love Words	47
	A Mink, a Fink, a Skating Rink	67
	Miss Spider's New Car*	68
	My Little Sister Ate One Hare*	78
	Summer Stinks	100
-ale (as in sale)	*My Daddy and I*	75
-alk	*Hello School!*	42
-all(s*)	*Belly Button Boy*	26
	Birds Build Nests	28
	Follow Me!	36
	Green Wilma	40
	House Mouse, Senate Mouse	44
	If I Ran the Rain Forest	50
	I'll Teach My Dog 100 Words	52
	Inchworm and a Half	54
	Loud Lips Lucy	61
	Marshall, the Courthouse Mouse	65
	More M&M's® Brand Math	69
	The Mouse Before Christmas	72
	My Daddy and I*	75
	My Hippie Grandmother	77

* indicates ending appears in the book

Spelling Patterns Matched to Books

Word Family	Book(s)	Lesson Page
-all(s*) (cont'd)	*The Night Before Valentine's Day*	85
	Put Me in the Zoo	90
	A Rainbow of Friends	93
	This Is the Sea that Feeds Us	102
	Wild About Books	110
	The Wolf's Story	111
	Woodrow, the White House Mouse	112
	Worry Wart Wes	113
-am	*Hello School!*	42
	Miss Spider's New Car	68
	Mr. Wiggle's Book	74
-ame(s*)	*Angel Pig and the Hidden Christmas**	23
	The Brand New Kid	29
	I Love Words	47
	Loud Lips Lucy	61
	Mr. Wiggle's Book	74
	Mystery Mansion	79
	The Night Before Summer Vacation	83
	The Night Before Valentine's Day	85
	Skittles® Riddles Math	97
	The Thingumajig Book of Manners	101
	'Twas the Night Before Thanksgiving	106
	Yikes—Lice!	114
-an	*Angel Pig and the Hidden Christmas*	23
	If I Ran the Rain Forest	50
	If the Shoe Fits	51
	Today Is Thanksgiving	104

* indicates ending appears in the book

Spelling Patterns Matched to Books

Word Family	Book(s)	Lesson Page
-ance	Counting Is for the Birds	31
	Giraffes Can't Dance	38
	Wild About Books	110
-and(s*)	Belly Button Boy	26
	Birds Build Nests	28
	How I Spent My Summer Vacation	45
	How Many, How Many, How Many	46
	In 1492	53
	Marshall, the Courthouse Mouse	65
	A Mink, a Fink, a Skating Rink	67
	More M&M's® Brand Math	69
	More Parts	70
	The Mouse Before Christmas	72
	My Daddy and I	75
	The Rules*	94
	This Is the Sea that Feeds Us	102
-andy	The M&M's® Brand Color Pattern Book	62
	More M&M's® Brand Math	69
-ang	'Twas the Day AFTER Thanksgiving	105
-ange	The Brand New Kid	29
-anger(s*)	Motherlove*	71
	Sleepless Beauty	98
-angled	Angel Pig and the Hidden Christmas	23

* indicates ending appears in the book

124

Spelling Patterns Matched to Books

Word Family	Book(s)	Lesson Page
-ant(s*)	*My Little Sister Ate One Hare**	78
-ap(s*, ping**)	*Angel Pig and the Hidden Christmas***	23
	Lizards for Lunch**	60
	The Night Before Kindergarten*	81
	The Night Before the Night Before Christmas	82
-ape(s*)	*The Night Before Valentine's Day**	85
	Parts	89
	Wild About Books	110
-appy	*Rumble in the Jungle*	95
-ar(s*)	*Angel Pig and the Hidden Christmas**	23
	The Brand New Kid	29
	I Love You, Mom	49
	A Mink, a Fink, a Skating Rink	67
	Miss Spider's New Car	68
	Mr. Monopoly's Amusement Park*	73
	My Daddy and I*	75
	My Hippie Grandmother	77
	The Night Before Kindergarten*	81
	This Is the Way We Go to School	103
-arch	*How Many, How Many, How Many*	46
-ard	*Bear Wants More*	25
	The Best Vacation Ever	27
-are(d*)	*Belly Button Boy*	26

* indicates ending appears in the book

** indicates ending appears in the book

Spelling Patterns Matched to Books

Word Family	Book(s)	Lesson Page
-are(d*) (cont'd)	Counting Is for the Birds	31
	The M&M's® Brand Counting Book	63
	The Night Before Kindergarten*	81
	The Night Before the Night Before Christmas	82
	A Rainbow of Friends	93
-arge	Hello School!	42
	Marshall, the Courthouse Mouse	65
	Woodrow, the White House Mouse	112
-ark	Birds Build Nests	28
	The Grumpy Morning	41
	Loud Lips Lucy	61
	Quick as a Cricket	91
-arm(ed*, s**)	The Brand New Kid**	29
	If I Ran the Rain Forest*	50
	Sleepless Beauty	98
-art	Marshall, the Courthouse Mouse	65
	More Parts	70
	The Night Before Easter	80
	Woodrow, the White House Mouse	112
-ash	Green Wilma	40
	Marshall, the Courthouse Mouse	65
	Mr. Monopoly's Amusement Park	73
	The Wedding	108

* indicates ending appears in the book

** indicates ending appears in the book

126

Spelling Patterns Matched to Books

Word Family	Book(s)	Lesson Page
-ass	*The Brand New Kid*	29
	House Mouse, Senate Mouse	44
	Today Is Thanksgiving	104
-ast	*Counting Is for the Birds*	31
	Little Miss Spider	59
	The M&M's® Brand Counting Book	63
	The Night Before Summer Vacation	83
	This Is the Way We Go to School	103
-at(s*)	*Angel Pig and the Hidden Christmas**	23
	The Flea's Sneeze	35
	How I Spent My Summer Vacation	45
	I Love You, Mom	49
	If the Shoe Fits	51
	I'll Teach My Dog 100 Words	52
	Loud Lips Lucy	61
	A Mink, a Fink, a Skating Rink	67
	*My Little Sister Ate One Hare**	78
	*The Night Before Summer Vacation**	83
	Put Me in the Zoo	90
	Sleepless Beauty	98
	Wild About Books	110
	Worry Wart Wes	113
	Yikes—Lice!	114
-atch	*Counting Is for the Birds*	31
	Itchy, Itchy Chicken Pox	55
	Lizards for Lunch	60

* indicates ending appears in the book

Rounding Up the Rhymes • Grades 1–3

Spelling Patterns Matched to Books

Word Family	Book(s)	Lesson Page
-ate(s*)	*Counting Is for the Birds*	31
	*House Mouse, Senate Mouse**	44
	The Library	58
	Marshall, the Courthouse Mouse	65
	The Wedding	108
-ath	*More M&M 's® Brand Math*	69
-ation(s*)	*Hooray for You!**	43
	If I Ran the Rain Forest	50
	Marshall, the Courthouse Mouse	65
	Mystery Mansion	79
	The Night Before Summer Vacation	83
	Oh, How I Wished I Could Read!	86
	Sleepless Beauty	98
	Woodrow, the White House Mouse	112
-atter(ed*)	*Don't Call Me Pig!*	33
	The Night Before Easter	80
	*The Night Before the Night Before Christmas**	82
	The Night Before Summer Vacation	83
	'Twas the Night Before Thanksgiving	106
-ave	*Woodrow, the White House Mouse*	112
-aw(s*)	*The Brand New Kid*	29
	Little Miss Spider	59
	*Rumble in the Jungle**	95
	'Twas the Night Before Thanksgiving	106
	The Wolf's Story	111

* indicates ending appears in the book

128

Spelling Patterns Matched to Books

Word Family	Book(s)	Lesson Page
-awn	*The Night Before Easter*	80
-ax(es*)	*A Mink, a Fink, a Skating Rink**	67
-ay(s*)	*Angel Pig and the Hidden Christmas*	23
	Belly Button Boy	26
	The Brand New Kid	29
	*Butterflies Fly**	30
	Counting Is for the Birds	31
	The Crayon Box that Talked	32
	Follow Me!	36
	Hello School!	42
	Hooray for You!	43
	House Mouse, Senate Mouse	44
	How I Spent My Summer Vacation	45
	I Love Words	47
	I Love You, Mom	49
	If I Ran the Rain Forest	50
	I'll Teach My Dog 100 Words	52
	In 1492	53
	Itchy, Itchy Chicken Pox	55
	The Library	58
	Loud Lips Lucy	61
	Many Luscious Lollipops	64
	A Mink, a Fink, a Skating Rink	67
	More Parts	70
	My Daddy and I	75
	My Grandpa and I	76

* indicates ending appears in the book

Spelling Patterns Matched to Books

Word Family	Book(s)	Lesson Page
-ay(s*) (cont'd)	*My Hippie Grandmother*	77
	Mystery Mansion	79
	The Night Before Easter	80
	The Night Before Kindergarten	81
	The Night Before Valentine's Day	85
	Oh, How I Wished I Could Read!	86
	Put Me in the Zoo	90
	A Rainbow of Friends	93
	The Rules	94
	Sleepless Beauty	98
	Summer Stinks	100
	The Thingumajig Book of Manners	101
	This Is the Sea that Feeds Us	102
	This Is the Way We Go to School	103
	Today Is Thanksgiving	104
	'Twas the Night Before Thanksgiving	106
	The Way I Feel	107
	The Wedding	108
	Wild About Books	110
	The Wolf's Story	111
	Woodrow, the White House Mouse	112
	Worry Wart Wes	113
	Yikes—Lice!	114
-aze	*Mystery Mansion*	79
-e	*Hooray for You!*	43
	I Love Words	47
	I Love You, Mom	49

* indicates ending appears in the book

Spelling Patterns Matched to Books

Word Family	Book(s)	Lesson Page
-e (cont'd)	*Inchworm and a Half*	54
	Loud Lips Lucy	61
	Oh, How I Wished I Could Read!	86
	Parts	89
	Put Me in the Zoo	90
	Summer Stinks	100
	The Way I Feel	107
	The Wedding	108
-ead (as in head)	*Hello School!*	42
	If I Ran the Rain Forest	50
	If the Shoe Fits	51
	The Library	58
	'Twas the Night Before Thanksgiving	106
-eak	*Parts*	89
	The Mouse Before Christmas	72
-eaker	*House Mouse, Senate Mouse*	44
-eal	*Belly Button Boy*	26
	The Grumpy Morning	41
	If I Ran the Rain Forest	50
-eam(s*)	*Butterflies Fly**	30
	How Many, How Many, How Many	46
	Loud Lips Lucy	61
	The Night Before the Night Before Christmas	82
	Oh, How I Wished I Could Read!	86
	Rabbit's Pajama Party	92
	Today Is Thanksgiving	104

* indicates ending appears in the book

Rounding Up the Rhymes • Grades 1–3

Spelling Patterns Matched to Books

Word Family	Book(s)	Lesson Page
-ean(s*)	*My Hippie Grandmother**	77
-ear (as in year), (s*)	*Angel Pig and the Hidden Christmas*	23
	The Bear Came Over to My House	24
	Don't Call Me Pig!	33
	*House Mouse, Senate Mouse**	44
	How Many, How Many, How Many	46
	I Love You Because You're You	48
	*If I Ran the Rain Forest**	50
	*Inchworm and a Half**	54
	Jennifer Jones Won't Leave Me Alone	57
	Loud Lips Lucy	61
	Marshall, the Courthouse Mouse	65
	More Parts	70
	The Night Before Easter	80
	The Night Before the Night Before Christmas	82
	The Night Before Summer Vacation	83
	The Night Before Valentine's Day	85
	Parts	89
	Rumble in the Jungle	95
-ease (as in please)	*The Brand New Kid*	29
-east(s*)	*Counting Is for the Birds*	31
	If the Shoe Fits	51
	Many Luscious Lollipops	64
	*'Twas the Night Before Thanksgiving**	106
-easure(s*)	*Inchworm and a Half**	54
	The Night Before Easter	80

* indicates ending appears in the book

Spelling Patterns Matched to Books

* indicates ending appears in the book

Spelling Patterns Matched to Books

Word Family	Book(s)	Lesson Page
-ee (cont'd)	*The Mouse Before Christmas*	72
	Mystery Mansion	79
	The Night Before the Night Before Christmas	82
	Over in the Garden	87
	Over in the Meadow	88
	Put Me in the Zoo	90
	The Wedding	108
	Woodrow, the White House Mouse	112
-eed(ed*, s**)	*Belly Button Boy*	26
	*Follow Me!***	36
	Hooray for You!	43
	Skittles® Riddles Math	97
	*The Wedding**	108
	Where Once There Was a Wood	109
-eek(ing*, s**)	*The Bear Came Over to My House*	24
	Follow Me!	36
	*Today Is Thanksgiving***	104
	*Woodrow, the White House Mouse**	112
-eel	*Giraffes Can't Dance*	38
-een	*The Crayon Box that Talked*	32
	I'll Teach My Dog 100 Words	52
	It's St. Patrick's Day	56
	The M&M's® Brand Color Pattern Book	62
	The M&M's® Brand Counting Book	63
	Skittles® Riddles Math	97

* indicates ending appears in the book

** indicates ending appears in the book

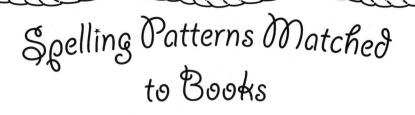

Spelling Patterns Matched to Books

* indicates ending appears in the book

** indicates ending appears in the book

Spelling Patterns Matched to Books

Word Family	Book(s)	Lesson Page
-ell(s*)	*The Brand New Kid*	29
	Don't Call Me Pig	33
	I Love Words	47
	*Miss Spider's New Car**	68
	The Night Before Summer Vacation	83
	Today Is Thanksgiving	104
	Wild About Books	110
-ella	*Marshall, the Courthouse Mouse*	65
-elly	*'Twas the Day AFTER Thanksgiving*	105
-elter	*If the Shoe Fits*	51
-elve(s*)	*Wild About Books**	110
-em	*If I Ran the Rain Forest*	50
-en	*Bear Wants More*	25
	The Grumpy Morning	41
	I Love Words	47
	If the Shoe Fits	51
	I'll Teach My Dog 100 Words	52
	The M&M's® Brand Counting Book	63
	Over in the Meadow	88
	The Shape of Things	96
	Somewhere in the Ocean	99
-end	*Inchworm and a Half*	54
	Mr. Monopoly's Amusement Park	73

* indicates ending appears in the book

Spelling Patterns Matched to Books

Word Family	Book(s)	Lesson Page
-ent(s*)	*My Grandpa and I*	76
	The Night Before Summer Vacation	83
	*Woodrow, the White House Mouse**	112
-enty	*More M&M's® Brand Math*	69
	Skittles® Riddles Math	97
-er	*Angel Pig and the Hidden Christmas*	23
	Loud Lips Lucy	61
	Sleepless Beauty	98
-ere (as in there)	*Worry Wart Wes*	113
-ero	*The M&M's® Brand Counting Book*	63
	Skittles® Riddles Math	97
-erry	*The Night Before Easter*	80
	This Is the Way We Go to School	103
-ese	*A Mink, a Fink, a Skating Rink*	67
-ess(ing*, ed**)	*Angel Pig and the Hidden Christmas*	23
	The Brand New Kid	29
	House Mouse, Senate Mouse	44
	Many Luscious Lollipops	64
	Marshall, the Courthouse Mouse	65
	My Little Sister Ate One Hare	78
	Sleepless Beauty	98
	*Today Is Thanksgiving**	104
	Woodrow, the White House Mouse	112
	*Worry Wart Wes***	113

* indicates ending appears in the book

** indicates ending appears in the book

Spelling Patterns Matched to Books

Word Family	Book(s)	Lesson Page
-est	*The 10 Best Things About My Dad*	22
	The Best Vacation Ever	27
	How I Spent My Summer Vacation	45
	If I Ran the Rain Forest	50
	If the Shoe Fits	51
	Little Miss Spider	59
	Lizards for Lunch	60
	Many Luscious Lollipops	64
	The Night Before the Night Before Christmas	82
	Rabbit's Pajama Party	92
	Rumble in the Jungle	95
-et	*Angel Pig and the Hidden Christmas*	23
	The Bear Came Over to My House	24
	If I Ran the Rain Forest	50
	The M&M's® Brand Counting Book	63
	More M&M's® Brand Math	69
	The Night Before Kindergarten	81
-ether	*Hello School!*	42
-etter	*House Mouse, Senate Mouse*	44
	Many Luscious Lollipops	64
-etto	*This Is the Way We Go to School*	103
-ew	*'Twas the Day AFTER Thanksgiving*	105
	Where Once There Was a Wood	109
-ext	*Marshall, the Courthouse Mouse*	65

Spelling Patterns Matched to Books

Word Family	Book(s)	Lesson Page
-ibe	*Hooray for You!*	43
-ice (as in ice)	*House Mouse, Senate Mouse*	44
	In 1492	53
	Inchworm and a Half	54
	Marshall, the Courthouse Mouse	65
	Miss Spider's New Car	68
	Mr. Wiggle's Book	74
	My Little Sister Ate One Hare	78
	Sleepless Beauty	98
	The Wedding	108
	Worry Wart Wes	113
	Yikes—Lice!	114
-ick(s*)	*How I Spent My Summer Vacation**	45
	How Many, How Many, How Many	46
	The Mouse Before Christmas	72
	Today Is Thanksgiving	104
	*The Wolf's Story**	111
	Worry Wart Wes	113
	Yikes—Lice!	114
-ickle	*Worry Wart Wes*	113
-icky	*If I Ran the Rain Forest*	50
	The Thingumajig Book of Manners	101
-id	*The Brand New Kid*	29
-iddle	*It's St. Patrick's Day!*	56

* indicates ending appears in the book

Spelling Patterns Matched to Books

Word Family	Book(s)	Lesson Page
-ide	*Bear Wants More*	25
	Birds Build Nests	28
	Hello School!	42
	I Love You, Mom	49
	If I Ran the Rain Forest	50
	Loud Lips Lucy	61
	The M&M's® Brand Counting Book	63
	Marshall, the Courthouse Mouse	65
	More M&M's® Brand Math	69
	The Mouse Before Christmas	72
	Mr. Monopoly's Amusement Park	73
	Mystery Mansion	79
	The Night Before Summer Vacation	83
	This Is the Way We Go to School	103
	The Wedding	108
	Woodrow, the White House Mouse	112
	Worry Wart Wes	113
-ie (as in pie), (s*)	*Many Luscious Lollipops**	64
	The Wolf's Story	111
-ied (as in cried)	*Miss Spider's New Car*	68
-ife	*Worry Wart Wes*	113
-ific	*Many Luscious Lollipops*	64
-ig(s*)	*Don't Call Me Pig!*	33
	I Love Words	47
	Little Miss Spider	59
	*The Thingumajig Book of Manners**	101

* indicates ending appears in the book

Spelling Patterns Matched to Books

Word Family	Book(s)	Lesson Page
-igh	*The Mouse Before Christmas*	72
-ight(s*)	*The 10 Best Things About My Dad*	22
	*Angel Pig and the Hidden Christmas**	23
	Bear Wants More	25
	Birds Build Nests	28
	The Brand New Kid	29
	Butterflies Fly	30
	Counting Is for the Birds	31
	How I Spent My Summer Vacation	45
	I Love Words	47
	If the Shoe Fits	51
	I'll Teach My Dog 100 Words	52
	Little Miss Spider	59
	Loud Lips Lucy	61
	The M&M's® Brand Color Pattern Book	62
	*Marshall, the Courthouse Mouse**	65
	Miss Spider's New Car	68
	More Parts	70
	My Grandpa and I	76
	The Night Before Summer Vacation	83
	The Night Before Valentine's Day	85
	Rabbit's Pajama Party	92
	*Rumble in the Jungle**	95
	The Thingumajig Book of Manners	101
	'Twas the Night Before Thanksgiving	106
	The Way I Feel	107
	Where Once There Was a Wood	109

* indicates ending appears in the book

© Carson-Dellosa • CD-104101   Rounding Up the Rhymes • Grades 1–3

Spelling Patterns Matched to Books

Word Family	Book(s)	Lesson Page
-ight(s*) (cont'd)	*Wild About Books*	110
	Worry Wart Wes	113
-ike	*Marshall, the Courthouse Mouse*	65
	The Night Before Summer Vacation	83
-ild	*Sleepless Beauty*	98
-ile	*The Brand New Kid*	29
	I Love Words	47
	More M&M's® Brand Math	69
	The Night Before Kindergarten	81
	The Night Before the Tooth Fairy	84
-ill(ed*, s**)	*Counting Is for the Birds*	31
	Each Peach Pear Plum	34
	*Hello School!**	42
	House Mouse, Senate Mouse	44
	A Mink, a Fink, a Skating Rink	67
	Mr. Monopoly's Amusement Park	73
	This Is the Way We Go to School	103
	*Wild About Books***	110
	Woodrow, the White House Mouse	112
-ilt	*Angel Pig and the Hidden Christmas*	23
-im	*My Hippie Grandmother*	77
-ime	*Angel Pig and the Hidden Christmas*	23
-imp	*Quick as a Cricket*	91

* indicates ending appears in the book

** indicates ending appears in the book

Spelling Patterns Matched to Books

Word Family	Book(s)	Lesson Page
-in	*Counting Is for the Birds*	31
	Hello School!	42
	House Mouse, Senate Mouse	44
	I Love Words	47
	Lizards for Lunch	60
	The M&M's® Brand Color Pattern Book	62
	More Parts	70
	Mystery Mansion	79
	The Night Before the Tooth Fairy	84
	Rabbit's Pajama Party	92
	Sleepless Beauty	98
	Today Is Thanksgiving	104
-inch	*Inchworm and a Half*	54
-ind (as in kind)	*Get Up and Go!*	37
	Hello School!	42
	Hooray for You!	43
	If I Ran the Rain Forest	50
	Loud Lips Lucy	61
	The M&M's® Brand Counting Book	63
	More Parts	70
	Mr. Wiggle's Book	74
	Rumble in the Jungle	95
	The Shape of Things	96
	Wild About Books	110
-ine (as in dine)	*The 10 Best Things About My Dad*	22
	Get Up and Go!	37
	Jennifer Jones Won't Leave Me Alone	57

Rounding Up the Rhymes • Grades 1–3

Spelling Patterns Matched to Books

Word Family	Book(s)	Lesson Page
-ine (as in dine) (cont'd)	*The Library*	58
	The M&M's® Brand Color Pattern Book	62
	The M&M's® Brand Counting Book	63
	Miss Spider's New Car	68
	More M&M's® Brand Math	69
	My Hippie Grandmother	77
	The Night Before the Night Before Christmas	82
	The Night Before Valentine's Day	85
	Over in the Garden	87
	Over in the Meadow	88
	Somewhere in the Ocean	99
	This Is the Way We Go to School	103
-ine (as in machine)	*A Mink, a Fink, a Skating Rink*	67
-ing (ing*, s**)	*Angel Pig and the Hidden Christmas***	23
	The Bear Came Over to My House	24
	*Butterflies Fly***	30
	I Love Words	47
	*I Love You, Mom***	49
	The Library	58
	Loud Lips Lucy	61
	A Mink, a Fink, a Skating Rink	67
	*Miss Spider's New Car***	68
	*Motherlove**	71
	My Grandpa and I	76
	The Night Before the Tooth Fairy	84
	This Is the Way We Go to School	103

* indicates ending appears in the book

** indicates ending appears in the book

144

Spelling Patterns Matched to Books

Word Family	Book(s)	Lesson Page
-ink	*The Bear Came Over to My House*	24
	Follow Me!	36
	Hooray for You!	43
	House Mouse, Senate Mouse	44
	I'll Teach My Dog 100 Words	52
	Loud Lips Lucy	61
	A Mink, a Fink, a Skating Rink	67
	The Night Before the Tooth Fairy	84
	Summer Stinks	100
-ip(s*)	*Follow Me!*	36
	If the Shoe Fits	51
	*Loud Lips Lucy**	61
	A Mink, a Fink, a Skating Rink	67
	*'Twas the Day AFTER Thanksgiving**	105
-irt	*More Parts*	70
-ise (as in rise), (s*)	*House Mouse, Senate Mouse*	44
	*Mr. Monopoly's Amusement Park**	73
	The Night Before Kindergarten	81
-ish(es*)	*Follow Me!*	36
	*This Is the Sea that Feeds Us**	102
	'Twas the Day AFTER Thanksgiving	105
-ision	*Marshall, the Courthouse Mouse*	65
-iss	*Sleepless Beauty*	98

* indicates ending appears in the book

Spelling Patterns Matched to Books

Word Family	Book(s)	Lesson Page
-it	How I Spent My Summer Vacation	45
	Inchworm and a Half	54
	The M&M's® Brand Color Pattern Book	62
	The Night Before the Night Before Christmas	82
	The Thingumajig Book of Manners	101
-iting	Wild About Books	110
-itch(y*)	Each Peach Pear Plum	34
	Itchy, Itchy Chicken Pox*	55
	Sleepless Beauty	98
-ither	If I Ran the Rain Forest	50
-ition	Marshall, the Courthouse Mouse	65
-itten(s*)	Goodnight Moon*	39
-ive (as in dive)	Counting Is for the Birds	31
	The Night Before the Night Before Christmas	82
	Over in the Garden	87
	Over in the Meadow	88
	Somewhere in the Ocean	99
-iver(s*) (as in giver)	The Mouse Before Christmas	72
	Rumble in the Jungle*	95
-iving (as in giving)	'Twas the Night Before Thanksgiving	106
-ix	The M&M's® Brand Color Pattern Book	62
	The M&M's® Brand Counting Book	63

* indicates ending appears in the book

Spelling Patterns Matched to Books

Word Family	Book(s)	Lesson Page
-ix (cont'd)	*Over in the Garden*	87
	Somewhere in the Ocean	99
-o (as in do)	*I'll Teach My Dog 100 Words*	52
	Inchworm and a Half	54
	Put Me in the Zoo	90
-o (as in go)	*I Love Words*	47
-oast	*I Love You, Mom*	49
-oaster(s*)	*The Night Before Summer Vacation**	83
-oat	*If the Shoe Fits*	51
	A Mink, a Fink, a Skating Rink	67
	This Is the Way We Go to School	103
-ock(ing*, s**)	*Goodnight Moon***	39
	If the Shoe Fits	51
	A Mink, a Fink, a Skating Rink	67
	*The Night Before the Night Before Christmas**	82
	Sleepless Beauty	98
-og(s*)	*The Flea's Sneeze*	35
	Green Wilma	40
	The Grumpy Morning	41
	Miss Spider's New Car	68
	*My Little Sister Ate One Hare**	78
-oice	*Angel Pig and the Hidden Christmas*	23
	Loud Lips Lucy	61

* indicates ending appears in the book

** indicates ending appears in the book

147

Rounding Up the Rhymes • Grades 1–3

Spelling Patterns Matched to Books

Word Family	Book(s)	Lesson Page
-ointment	*Oh, How I Wished I Could Read!*	86
-oke	*Sleepless Beauty*	98
-old	*Birds Build Nests*	28
	In 1492	53
	Worry Wart Wes	113
-ole(s*)	*Bear Wants More*	25
	*Miss Spider's New Car**	68
	Mystery Mansion	79
-ome (as in dome)	*Jennifer Jones Won't Leave Me Alone*	57
-ond	*Green Wilma*	40
-one (as in done)	*Get Up and Go!*	37
	Hooray for You!	43
	I Love Words	47
	Inchworm and a Half	54
	The M&M's® Brand Color Pattern Book	62
	Marshall, the Courthouse Mouse	65
	Miss Spider's New Car	68
	More M&M's® Brand Math	69
	The Night Before Easter	80
	The Night Before Valentine's Day	85
	Skittles® Riddles Math	97
-one (as in bone)	*How Many, How Many, How Many*	46
	I'll Teach My Dog 100 Words	52
	The M&M's® Brand Counting Book	63

* indicates ending appears in the book

Spelling Patterns Matched to Books

Word Family	Book(s)	Lesson Page
-ong	*The 10 Best Things About My Dad*	22
	The Crayon Box that Talked	32
	Inchworm and a Half	54
	It's St. Patrick's Day!	56
	Lizards for Lunch	60
	Marshall, the Courthouse Mouse	65
	The Night Before the Night Before Christmas	82
	The Wedding	108
	The Wolf's Story	111
-on't	*I Love Words*	47
-oo	*Angel Pig and the Hidden Christmas*	23
	How I Spent My Summer Vacation	45
	Put Me in the Zoo	90
	Yikes—Lice!	114
-ood (as in wood)	*Belly Button Boy*	26
	Counting Is for the Birds	31
	Each Peach Pear Plum	34
	The Wolf's Story	111
-ood (as in food)	*Angel Pig and the Hidden Christmas*	23
	Where Once There Was a Wood	109
	Yikes—Lice!	114
-oodle	*A Mink, a Fink, a Skating Rink*	67
-ook(s*)	*Angel Pig and the Hidden Christmas**	23
	*The Brand New Kid**	29
	I Love Words	47

* indicates ending appears in the book

Spelling Patterns Matched to Books

Word Family	Book(s)	Lesson Page
-ook(s*) (cont'd)	*I Love You, Mom*	49
	The Library	58
	Loud Lips Lucy	61
	The M&M's® Brand Color Pattern Book	62
	*Marshall, the Courthouse Mouse**	65
	The Thingumajig Book of Manners	101
	This Is the Sea that Feeds Us	102
	*Wild About Books**	110
	Yikes—Lice!	114
-ool	*The Brand New Kid*	29
	Loud Lips Lucy	61
	The Night Before Kindergarten	81
	Sleepless Beauty	98
	This Is the Way We Go to School	103
-oom(s*, y**)	*Angel Pig and the Hidden Christmas*	23
	Belly Button Boy	26
	Hello School!	42
	*If I Ran the Rain Forest**	50
	More Parts	70
	Sleepless Beauty	98
	*The Wedding***	108
-oon	*Goodnight Moon*	39
	House Mouse, Senate Mouse	44
	Jennifer Jones Won't Leave Me Alone	57
-oop	*Inchworm and a Half*	54

* indicates ending appears in the book

** indicates ending appears in the book

Spelling Patterns Matched to Books

Word Family	Book(s)	Lesson Page
-oor(s*)	*Angel Pig and the Hidden Christmas**	23
	The Library	58
	Miss Spider's New Car	68
	The Mouse Before Christmas	72
	The Night Before the Night Before Christmas	82
-oose	*I'll Teach My Dog 100 Words*	52
-op(s*, ping**)	*I Love Words*	47
	I Love You, Mom	49
	The M&M's® Brand Counting Book	63
	*Many Luscious Lollipops**	64
	*The Night Before Easter**	80
	*The Night Before the Night Before Christmas***	82
	The Wedding	108
	Yikes—Lice!	114
-ope	*A Mink, a Fink, a Skating Rink*	67
-ore	*Bear Wants More*	25
	The Brand New Kid	29
	Hello School!	42
	Hooray for You!	43
	I Love You, Mom	49
	Inchworm and a Half	54
	Jennifer Jones Won't Leave Me Alone	57
	Loud Lips Lucy	61
	Many Luscious Lollipops	64
	Motherlove	71

* indicates ending appears in the book

** indicates ending appears in the book

Spelling Patterns Matched to Books

Word Family	Book(s)	Lesson Page
-ore (cont'd)	*Worry Wart Wes*	113
	Yikes—Lice!	114
-orn	*The Brand New Kid*	29
	It's St. Patrick's Day!	56
-ort	*If I Ran the Rain Forest*	50
	Summer Stinks	100
-ose	*Many Luscious Lollipops*	64
	The Night Before Easter	80
-ost (as in post)	*Mr. Monopoly's Amusement Park*	73
-ost (as in cost)	*My Grandpa and I*	76
-ot(s*)	*The Best Vacation Ever*	27
	Giraffes Can't Dance	38
	House Mouse, Senate Mouse	44
	*If I Ran the Rain Forest**	50
	In 1492	53
	*Inchworm and a Half**	54
	*Itchy, Itchy Chicken Pox**	55
	Jennifer Jones Won't Leave Me Alone	57
	Mr. Monopoly's Amusement Park	73
	Rumble in the Jungle	95
	Summer Stinks	100
	The Wolf's Story	111

* indicates ending appears in the book

Spelling Patterns Matched to Books

Word Family	Book(s)	Lesson Page
-ote	*Marshall, the Courthouse Mouse*	65
	Miss Spider's New Car	68
	Woodrow, the White House Mouse	112
-other(s*)	*Hooray for You!*	43
	If I Ran the Rain Forest	50
	*The Thingumajig Book of Manners**	101
-otion	*Many Luscious Lollipops*	64
-otter	*Wild About Books*	110
-ouch	*Sleepless Beauty*	98
-oud	*Butterflies Fly*	30
	I Love You, Mom	49
	Loud Lips Lucy	61
	Rumble in the Jungle	95
-ould	*The M&M's® Brand Counting Book*	63
	Worry Wart Wes	113
-ound(s*)	*Bear Wants More*	25
	Counting Is for the Birds	31
	Giraffes Can't Dance	38
	How I Spent My Summer Vacation	45
	I Love Words	47
	I Love You Because You're You	48
	If I Ran the Rain Forest	50
	Lizards for Lunch	60
	Loud Lips Lucy	61

* indicates ending appears in the book

Spelling Patterns Matched to Books

* indicates ending appears in the book

Spelling Patterns Matched to Books

Word Family	Book(s)	Lesson Page
-out	*Angel Pig and the Hidden Christmas*	23
	Belly Button Boy	26
	The Best Vacation Ever	27
	Counting Is for the Birds	31
	Hello School!	42
	Hooray for You!	43
	I Love You Because You're You	48
	Loud Lips Lucy	61
	The Mouse Before Christmas	72
	Mystery Mansion	79
	The Night Before the Night Before Christmas	82
	The Night Before the Tooth Fairy	84
	Parts	89
	The Wolf's Story	111
-ove (as in love), (ing*, s**)	*The 10 Best Things About My Dad**	22
	Angel Pig and the Hidden Christmas	23
	Giraffes Can't Dance	38
	If the Shoe Fits	51
	Motherlove	71
	'Twas the Night Before Thanksgiving	106
-ove (as in move), (d*)	*Woodrow, the White House Mouse**	112
-over	*It's St. Patrick's Day!*	56

* indicates ending appears in the book

** indicates ending appears in the book

Spelling Patterns Matched to Books

Word Family	Book(s)	Lesson Page
-ow (as in snow), (ing*, s**)	Angel Pig and the Hidden Christmas**	23
	Belly Button Boy	26
	Hooray for You!	43
	I Love Words	47
	If I Ran the Rain Forest	50
	The M&M's® Brand Counting Book	63
	Miss Spider's New Car*	68
	More M&M's® Brand Math	69
	Motherlove	71
	Oh, How I Wished I Could Read!	86
	The Thingumajig Book of Manners	101
	This Is the Way We Go to School	103
-ow (as in cow), (s*)	Giraffes Can't Dance	38
	The Grumpy Morning	41
	I Love Words	47
	Itchy, Itchy Chicken Pox	55
	The M&M's® Brand Counting Book	63
	Motherlove*	71
	The Night Before Kindergarten	81
-ower	Miss Spider's New Car	68
	My Hippie Grandmother	77
-owl	The Flea's Sneeze	35
	Rumble in the Jungle	95
-own (as in town)	Birds Build Nests	28
	I Love You, Mom	49

* indicates ending appears in the book

** indicates ending appears in the book

Spelling Patterns Matched to Books

Word Family	Book(s)	Lesson Page
-own (as in town) (cont'd)	*I'll Teach My Dog 100 Words*	52
	The M&M's® Brand Color Pattern Book	62
	Many Luscious Lollipops	64
	A Mink, a Fink, a Skating Rink	67
	Miss Spider's New Car	68
	The Mouse Before Christmas	72
	Sleepless Beauty	98
	This Is the Sea that Feeds Us	102
	The Wedding	108
-ox	*I Love Words*	47
	Quick as a Cricket	91
-oy(s*)	*The Night Before Valentine's Day**	85
	*The Thingumajig Book of Manners**	101
	The Wedding	108
-ub	*If the Shoe Fits*	51
-uck	*Bear Wants More*	25
	The Grumpy Morning	41
	I Love You, Mom	49
-ucky	*Itchy, Itchy Chicken Pox*	55
-uddle	*Motherlove*	71
-ue(s*)	*If I Ran the Rain Forest*	50
	*Motherlove**	71

* indicates ending appears in the book

Spelling Patterns Matched to Books

Word Family	Book(s)	Lesson Page
-uff(ing*, ed**)	*A Mink a Fink, a Skating Rink*	67
	*'Twas the Night Before Thanksgiving**	106
	*The Wolf's Story***	111
-ug(s*)	*I Love You Because You're You*	48
	The Night Before Kindergarten	81
	*Yikes—Lice!**	114
-um	*Hello School!*	42
	If I Ran the Rain Forest	50
-umber	*Inchworm and a Half*	54
-umble	*Hello School!*	42
	The Mouse Before Christmas	72
	Mystery Mansion	79
-ummer	*Summer Stinks*	100
-ummy	*Bear Wants More*	25
-ump	*The Grumpy Morning*	41
	I Love Words	47
	Miss Spider's New Car	68
-un	*Don't Call Me Pig!*	33
	How Many, How Many, How Many	46
	Skittles® Riddles Math	97
-unch(es*)	*Bear Wants More*	25
	Lizards for Lunch	60

* indicates ending appears in the book

** indicates ending appears in the book

Spelling Patterns Matched to Books

Word Family	Book(s)	Lesson Page
-unch(es*) (cont'd)	*More M&M's® Brand Math*	69
	Wild About Books*	110
-unk	*The Library*	58
-unny	*Hello School!*	42
	The Night Before Easter	80
-unt(ing*)	*Each Peach Pear Plum**	34
-up	*Belly Button Boy*	26
	If the Shoe Fits	51
	I'll Teach My Dog 100 Words	52
-urry	*Motherlove*	71
-ush	*Goodnight Moon*	39
-using	*Skittles® Riddles Math*	97
-ut	*Hello School!*	42
-ution	*House Mouse, Senate Mouse*	44
	Marshall, the Courthouse Mouse	65
-utter(s*)	*Angel Pig and the Hidden Christmas*	23
	The Night Before the Night Before Christmas*	82
-y	*Butterflies Fly*	30
	The Crayon Box that Talked	32
	Get Up and Go!	37

* indicates ending appears in the book

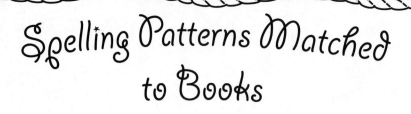

Spelling Patterns Matched to Books

Spelling Patterns with Transfer Words

-able able, cable, fable, label, sable, stable, table, disable, enable, mislabel, timetable, unable, unstable

-ace ace, brace, face, grace, lace, pace, place, race, space, trace, birthplace, bookcase, briefcase, deface, disgrace, embrace, fireplace, misplace, replace, retrace, shoelace, unlace, workplace, anyplace

-ack back, black, crack, flack, hack, jack, knack, lack, pack, quack, rack, sack, shack, slack, smack, snack, stack, tack, track, whack, attack, backpack, backtrack, feedback, flapjack, flashback, fullback, haystack, icepack, knapsack, setback, unpack, paperback, piggyback, quarterback

-act act, fact, pact, tact, tract, abstract, attract, compact, contract, distract, enact, exact, impact, react, transact, artifact, interact, overact, overreact

-ad ad, bad, Brad, cad, Chad, clad, dad, fad, grad, had, lad, mad, pad, sad, tad, doodad, egad, granddad, nomad, Sinbad, Galahad, ironclad, Trinidad, undergrad, Olympiad

-ade blade, fade, grade, jade, made, shade, spade, trade, wade, arcade, blockade, charade, crusade, decade, grenade, homemade, invade, lampshade, parade, persuade, tirade, unmade, upgrade, accolade, barricade, cavalcade, centigrade, escapade, Gatorade®, lemonade, marmalade, masquerade, promenade, renegade, serenade

-ag bag, brag, drag, flag, gag, jag, lag, nag, rag, sag, snag, stag, tag, wag, beanbag, dishrag, mailbag, sandbag, washrag, zigzag, litterbag, saddlebag

-age age, cage, page, rage, sage, stage, wage, backstage, engage, enrage, offstage, outrage, rampage, teenage, upstage

-ail ail, bail, fail, frail, hail, jail, mail, nail, pail, quail, rail, sail, snail, tail, trail, wail, airmail, blackmail, curtail, derail, detail, hangnail, pigtail, prevail, retail, shirttail, thumbnail, toenail, Abigail, cottontail, fingernail, monorail

-ain brain, chain, drain, gain, grain, main, pain, plain, rain, slain, Spain, sprain, stain, train, vain, abstain, birdbrain, complain, contain, disdain, domain, explain, maintain, obtain, refrain, regain, remain, restrain, retain, sustain, tearstain, terrain, unchain, ascertain, entertain, featherbrain, potty-train, scatterbrain

Spelling Patterns with Transfer Words

-air   air, chair, fair, flair, hair, lair, pair, stair, affair, despair, impair, midair, repair, unfair, wheelchair, debonair

-ake   bake, Blake, brake, cake, fake, flake, Jake, lake, make, quake, rake, sake, shake, snake, stake, take, wake, awake, cheesecake, clambake, cupcake, earthquake, fruitcake, handshake, intake, keepsake, mistake, namesake, pancake, remake, shortcake, snowflake, overtake, rattlesnake

-ale   (as in sale) ale, gale, male, pale, sale, scale, stale, tale, whale, Yale, exhale, female, inhale, telltale, upscale, wholesale, nightingale, tattletale

-alk   balk, chalk, stalk, talk, walk, beanstalk, boardwalk, crosswalk, jaywalk, outtalk, sidewalk, sleepwalk

-all   all, ball, call, fall, gall, hall, mall, small, squall, stall, tall, wall, appall, baseball, birdcall, downfall, enthrall, eyeball, football, goofball, handball, install, meatball, nightfall, oddball, pinball, pitfall, rainfall, recall, snowball, snowfall, spitball, stonewall, basketball, butterball, cannonball, overall, volleyball, waterfall

-am   am, clam, cram, dam, gram, ham, jam, Pam, ram, Sam, scam, scram, sham, slam, swam, tram, wham, yam, exam, flimflam, program, Abraham, Amsterdam, anagram, Birmingham, diagram, milligram, telegram

-ame   blame, came, dame, fame, flame, frame, game, lame, name, same, shame, tame, aflame, became, defame, inflame, nickname, surname, overcame

-an   an, ban, bran, can, clan, fan, Fran, Jan, man, Nan, pan, plan, ran, scan, span, Stan, tan, than, van, Batman®, began, cancan, caveman, dustpan, hangman, Japan, lawman, madman, outran, sandman, sedan, suntan, caravan, handyman, overran, Pakistan, Superman®, Afghanistan

-ance   chance, dance, France, glance, lance, prance, stance, trance, advance, enhance, entrance, finance, romance, circumstance

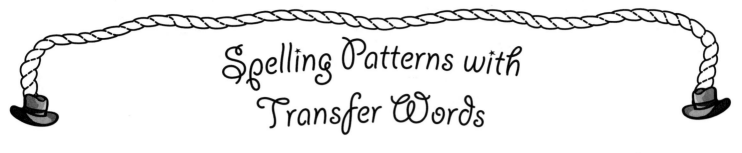

Spelling Patterns with Transfer Words

-and   and, band, bland, brand, gland, grand, hand, land, sand, stand, strand, armband, backhand, bandstand, command, cowhand, demand, disband, dreamland, expand, firsthand, grandstand, handstand, headband, homeland, kickstand, longhand, name-brand, offhand, quicksand, shorthand, Thailand, wasteland, beforehand, contraband, Disneyland®, Dixieland, fairyland, reprimand, secondhand, understand, fantasyland, misunderstand

-andy   Andy, candy, dandy, handy, Randy, sandy

-ang   bang, clang, dang, fang, gang, hang, rang, sang, slang, sprang, Tang®, twang, mustang, boomerang, overhang

-ange   change, range, strange, arrange, downrange, exchange, shortchange, interchange, prearrange, rearrange

-anger   danger, stranger, arranger, exchanger

-angle   angle, dangle, mangle, tangle, strangle, wrangle

-ant   ant, chant, grant, pant, plant, rant, scant, slant, eggplant, enchant, implant, supplant, transplant, disenchant, gallivant

-ap   cap, chap, clap, flap, gap, lap, map, nap, rap, sap, scrap, slap, snap, strap, tap, trap, wrap, yap, zap, burlap, catnap, firetrap, giftwrap, hubcap, kidnap, kneecap, mishap, mousetrap, recap, unwrap, wiretap, gingersnap, handicap, overlap

-ape   ape, cape, drape, gape, grape, scrape, shape, tape, agape, escape, landscape, reshape, shipshape

-appy   happy, pappy, sappy, scrappy, snappy, slaphappy, unhappy

Spelling Patterns with Transfer Words

-ar   bar, car, czar, far, jar, mar, par, scar, spar, star, tar, tsar, ajar, boxcar, cigar, costar, disbar, guitar, streetcar, handlebar, registrar, seminar, superstar, Zanzibar

-arch   arch, March, march, parch, starch

-ard   bard, card, hard, lard, yard, backyard, barnyard, Bernard, blowhard, bombard, diehard, discard, graveyard, junkyard, postcard, regard, scorecard, shipyard, boulevard, disregard, leotard

-are   bare, blare, care, dare, fare, flare, glare, hare, mare, rare, scare, share, snare, spare, square, stare, ware, airfare, aware, beware, compare, declare, fanfare, nightmare, prepare, threadbare, warfare, Delaware, silverware, unaware

-arge   barge, charge, large, Marge, discharge, enlarge, recharge, overcharge

-ark   ark, bark, Clark, dark, hark, lark, mark, park, shark, spark, stark, aardvark, ballpark, birthmark, bookmark, Denmark, earmark, footmark, landmark, postmark, remark, skylark, trademark, disembark

-arm   arm, charm, farm, harm, alarm, disarm, firearm, underarm

-art   art, cart, chart, dart, mart, part, smart, start, tart, apart, depart, impart, K-Mart®, Mozart, outsmart, restart, sweetheart

-ash   ash, bash, brash, cash, clash, crash, dash, flash, gash, gnash, hash, lash, mash, rash, sash, slash, smash, splash, stash, thrash, trash, backlash, eyelash, mishmash, whiplash, balderdash, succotash

-ass   bass, brass, class, crass, glass, grass, lass, mass, pass, sass, amass, bypass, harass, surpass, trespass, hourglass, overpass

Spelling Patterns with Transfer Words

-ast blast, cast, fast, last, mast, past, vast, aghast, broadcast, contrast, downcast, forecast, gymnast, miscast, newscast, outcast, outlast, sandblast, steadfast, typecast, flabbergast, overcast, telecast

-at at, bat, brat, cat, chat, fat, flat, gnat, hat, mat, pat, rat, sat, spat, splat, that, vat, chitchat, combat, dingbat, doormat, format, hardhat, muskrat, nonfat, tomcat, wildcat, wombat, acrobat, bureaucrat, democrat, diplomat, habitat, Laundromat®, thermostat, aristocrat

-atch batch, catch, hatch, latch, match, patch, scratch, snatch, thatch, dispatch, mismatch, unlatch,

-ate ate, crate, date, fate, gate, grate, hate, Kate, late, mate, plate, rate, skate, slate, state, birthrate, checkmate, classmate, Colgate®, create, debate, deflate, donate, elate, equate, estate, frustrate, helpmate, inflate, locate, mandate, migrate, narrate, ornate, playmate, primate, rebate, relate, rotate, sedate, stalemate, tailgate, translate, update, vacate, vibrate, activate, advocate, aggravate, agitate, allocate, amputate, animate, calculate, candidate, captivate, celebrate, circulate, complicate, concentrate, confiscate, contemplate, cultivate, decorate, dedicate, delegate, demonstrate, detonate, devastate, deviate, dislocate, dominate, duplicate, educate, elevate, emigrate, estimate, excavate, fascinate, formulate, fumigate, generate, graduate, gravitate, hesitate, hibernate, hyphenate, illustrate, imitate, immigrate, indicate, infiltrate, instigate, integrate, irrigate, irritate, isolate, legislate, liberate, liquidate, medicate, meditate, motivate, nauseate, navigate, nominate, operate, overate, overstate, populate, punctuate, radiate, regulate, segregate, separate, situate, speculate, stimulate, suffocate, terminate, tolerate, vaccinate, validate, violate, abbreviate, accelerate, accommodate, accumulate, alienate, anticipate, appreciate, associate, carbohydrate, communicate, congratulate, contaminate, cooperate, coordinate, discriminate, elaborate, eliminate, emancipate, evacuate, evaluate, evaporate, exaggerate, exterminate, hallucinate, humiliate, illuminate, impersonate, inoculate, interrogate, intimidate, investigate, officiate, participate, procrastinate, recuperate

Spelling Patterns with Transfer Words

-ath   bath, math, path, wrath, birdbath, warpath, aftermath

-ation   nation, station, creation, dictation, donation, duration, elation, formation, foundation, frustration, inflation, location, migration, plantation, probation, quotation, relation, rotation, starvation, summation, vacation, adaptation, admiration, aggravation, agitation, animation, application, aviation, calculation, cancellation, celebration, circulation, combination, complication, concentration, confirmation, congregation, consolation, conversation, corporation, declaration, decoration, dedication, dehydration, demonstration, desperation, destination, devastation, duplication, elevation, expectation, explanation, exploration, fabrication, fascination, generation, graduation, hesitation, illustration, imitation, immigration, inflammation, information, innovation, inspiration, integration, irritation, isolation, legislation, liberation, medication, moderation, motivation, nomination, obligation, occupation, operation, perspiration, population, preparation, presentation, preservation, punctuation, radiation, recreation, registration, regulation, relaxation, reputation, reservation, resignation, revelation, segregation, separation, situation, speculation, stimulation, transportation, vacation, variation, abbreviation, acceleration, anticipation, appreciation, assassination, civilization, communication, consideration, cooperation, coordination, determination, discrimination, elimination, evaluation, exasperation, extermination, hallucination, humiliation, imagination, impersonation, initiation, interpretation, interrogation, intimidation, intoxication, investigation, justification, manipulation, multiplication, notification, organization, participation, procrastination, pronunciation, qualification, realization, recommendation, retaliation, sophistication, verification

-atter   batter, chatter, clatter, fatter, flatter, latter, matter, platter, scatter, shatter, splatter, tatter

-ave   brave, cave, crave, gave, grave, knave, pave, rave, save, shave, slave, wave, behave, brainwave, engrave, forgave, shockwave, aftershave, microwave, misbehave

-aw   caw, claw, draw, flaw, gnaw, jaw, law, paw, raw, saw, slaw, straw, thaw, jigsaw, outdraw, outlaw, seesaw, withdraw

Spelling Patterns with Transfer Words

-awn   dawn, drawn, fawn, lawn, pawn, spawn, yawn, withdrawn, overdrawn

-ax   ax, fax, lax, sax, tax, wax, climax, earwax, relax

-ay   bay, bray, clay, day, fray, gay, gray, hay, lay, may, nay, pay, play, pray, ray, say, spray, stay, stray, sway, tray, way, away, birthday, decay, delay, display, essay, gangway, halfway, hallway, headway, highway, Norway, okay, railway, relay, repay, someway, stairway, stingray, subway, today, weekday, X-ray, everyday, faraway, holiday, runaway, stowaway, underway, yesterday

-aze   blaze, craze, daze, faze, gaze, glaze, graze, haze, laze, maze, ablaze, amaze, stargaze

-e   be, he, me, she, we

-ead   (as in head) bread, dead, dread, head, lead, read, spread, thread, tread, ahead, blockhead, forehead, hardhead, homestead, instead, misread, proofread, redhead, spearhead, widespread, arrowhead, gingerbread, letterhead, overhead, sleepyhead

-eak   beak, bleak, creak, freak, leak, peak, sneak, speak, squeak, streak, tweak, weak, misspeak, pip-squeak

-eaker   beaker, sneaker, speaker, weaker, loudspeaker

-eal   deal, heal, meal, real, seal, squeal, steal, teal, veal, zeal, appeal, conceal, congeal, ideal, misdeal, oatmeal, ordeal, reveal, unreal

-eam   beam, cream, dream, gleam, ream, scream, seam, steam, stream, team, bloodstream, daydream, downstream, mainstream, moonbeam, sunbeam

-ean   bean, clean, dean, glean, Jean, lean, mean

Spelling Patterns with Transfer Words

-ear   (as in year) clear, dear, ear, fear, gear, hear, near, rear, smear, spear, tear, year, appear, unclear, disappear, overhear, reappear

-ease   (as in please) ease, please, tease, disease

-east   beast, east, feast, least, yeast

-easure measure, pleasure, treasure, displeasure

-eat   beat, bleat, cheat, eat, feat, heat, meat, neat, pleat, seat, treat, wheat, backseat, browbeat, deadbeat, defeat, heartbeat, mistreat, repeat, retreat, upbeat, overeat

-eave   heave, leave, weave

-ect   sect, affect, collect, connect, correct, defect, detect, direct, dissect, effect, eject, elect, erect, expect, infect, inject, insect, inspect, neglect, object, perfect, project, prospect, protect, reflect, reject, respect, select, subject, suspect, architect, disconnect, disinfect, disrespect, incorrect, indirect, intellect, intersect, recollect, reelect

-ection section, affection, collection, conception, connection, correction, dejection, direction, ejection, election, infection, inflection, injection, inspection, objection, perfection, protection, reflection, rejection, selection, imperfection, interjection, intersection, recollection, resurrection

-ed   bed, bled, Ed, fed, fled, led, red, shed, shred, sled, sped, Ted, wed, bobsled, coed, moped, purebred, sickbed, spoon-fed, unwed, bottle-fed, infrared, newlywed, overfed, Sudafed®, thoroughbred, underfed, waterbed

-ee   bee, fee, flee, free, gee, glee, knee, see, spree, tee, three, tree, agree, carefree, degree, emcee, peewee, sightsee, teepee, absentee, bumblebee, chimpanzee, disagree, employee, guarantee, jamboree, nominee, oversee, pedigree, referee, refugee, Tennessee

Spelling Patterns with Transfer Words

-eed bleed, breed, creed, deed, feed, freed, greed, heed, kneed, need, reed, seed, speed, steed, treed, tweed, weed, agreed, exceed, indeed, nosebleed, proceed, seaweed, succeed, disagreed, guaranteed, overfeed, refereed, tumbleweed

-eek cheek, creek, geek, Greek, meek, peek, reek, seek, sleek, week, midweek

-eel eel, feel, heel, keel, kneel, peel, reel, steel, wheel, cartwheel, genteel, newsreel

-een green, keen, queen, screen, seen, sheen, teen, between, canteen, Colleen, eighteen, fifteen, fourteen, Kathleen, nineteen, preteen, seventeen, sixteen, smokescreen, sunscreen, thirteen, unseen, evergreen, Halloween

-eep beep, bleep, creep, deep, jeep, keep, peep, seep, sheep, sleep, steep, sweep, weep, asleep, oversleep

-ees bees, fees, flees, frees, knees, sees, sprees, trees, agrees, degrees, foresees, tepees, bumblebees, chickadees, chimpanzees, disagrees, dungarees, guarantees, jamborees, nominees, oversees, pedigrees, referees

-eet beet, feet, fleet, greet, meet, sheet, sleet, street, sweet, tweet, discreet, bittersweet, indiscreet, parakeet

-eeze breeze, freeze, sneeze, wheeze, antifreeze

-eg beg, Greg, keg, leg, Meg, peg, Winnipeg

-elf elf, self, shelf, bookshelf, herself, himself, itself, myself, yourself

-ell bell, cell, dwell, fell, jell, Nell, sell, shell, smell, spell, swell, tell, well, yell, bombshell, doorbell, eggshell, farewell, inkwell, Maxwell, misspell, nutshell, retell, unwell

-ella Della, Ella, fella, Stella, umbrella, Cinderella, Isabella, mozzarella

Spelling Patterns with Transfer Words

-elly	belly, jelly, Kelly, smelly, potbelly
-elter	shelter, smelter, swelter, helter-skelter
-elve	delve, shelve, twelve
-em	gem, hem, stem, them
-en	Ben, den, hen, men, pen, ten, then, when, yen, amen, bullpen, pigpen, playpen
-end	bend, blend, lend, mend, send, spend, tend, trend, amend, ascend, attend, defend, depend, descend, extend, intend, offend, pretend, suspend, transcend, unbend, upend, apprehend, comprehend, dividend, overspend, recommend
-ent	bent, cent, dent, gent, Lent, rent, scent, sent, spent, tent, vent, went, cement, consent, content, descent, dissent, event, extent, indent, intent, invent, lament, misspent, percent, present, prevent, repent, resent, torment, compliment, discontent, evident, implement, malcontent, represent, underwent, experiment, misrepresent
-enty	plenty, twenty
-er	her, per, confer, defer, deter, infer, prefer, refer
-ere	(as in there) there, where, elsewhere, nowhere, somewhere, anywhere, everywhere
-ero	hero, Nero, zero
-erry	berry, cherry, ferry, merry, Perry, Terry, blueberry, raspberry, strawberry, blackberry

Spelling Patterns with Transfer Words

-ess   Bess, bless, chess, dress, guess, less, mess, press, stress, Tess, access, address, caress, confess, depress, digress, distress, duress, excess, express, impress, oppress, outguess, possess, profess, progress, recess, regress, repress, success, suppress, undress, unless, nonetheless, repossess, nevertheless

-est   best, chest, crest, guest, jest, nest, pest, quest, rest, test, vest, west, zest, arrest, conquest, contest, detest, invest, protest, request, suggest, decongest, manifest

-et   bet, fret, get, jet, met, net, pet, set, vet, wet, whet, yet, cadet, dragnet, duet, forget, quartet, regret, reset, sunset, Tibet, upset, alphabet, bassinet, bayonet, clarinet, Juliet, minuet

-ether   tether, whether, together, altogether

-etter   better, letter, wetter, forgetter, newsletter, trendsetter

-etto   ghetto, falsetto, Gepetto, libretto, stiletto

-ew   blew, brew, chew, crew, dew, drew, few, flew, grew, knew, mew, new, pew, screw, slew, stew, threw, view, anew, cashew, curfew, outgrew, renew, review, withdrew, interview

-ext   next, text, context

-ibe   bribe, gibe, scribe, tribe, describe, imbibe, inscribe, prescribe, subscribe, transcribe, diatribe

-ice   as in ice) dice, ice, lice, mice, nice, price, rice, slice, spice, twice, vice, advice, device, entice, suffice, sacrifice

-ick   brick, chick, click, Dick, flick, kick, lick, nick, Nick, pick, prick, sick, slick, stick, thick, tick, trick, airsick, broomstick, chopstick, drumstick, handpick, heartsick, homesick, lipstick, lovesick, nitpick, seasick, sidekick, slapstick, toothpick, yardstick, candlestick

Spelling Patterns with Transfer Words

-ickle   fickle, pickle, sickle, tickle, trickle

-icky   icky, Nicky, picky, sticky, tricky, Vicky

-id   bid, did, grid, hid, id, kid, lid, rid, Sid, skid, slid, squid, amid, eyelid, forbid, hybrid, Madrid, outbid, outdid, redid, arachnid, overdid, pyramid

-iddle   diddle, fiddle, griddle, middle, piddle, riddle, twiddle

-ide   bride, chide, glide, hide, pride, ride, side, slide, snide, stride, tide, wide, aside, bedside, beside, chloride, collide, confide, decide, divide, fireside, inside, joyride, landslide, misguide, outside, provide, reside, riptide, roadside, subside, worldwide, coincide, insecticide

-ie   die, lie, pie, tie, vie, magpie, necktie, untie, underlie

-ied   (as in cried) cried, died, dried, fried, lied, pried, shied, spied, tied, tried, vied, applied, defied, denied, implied, relied, replied, supplied, untied, clarified, dignified, glorified, horrified, justified, magnified, modified, multiplied, notified, occupied, pacified, petrified, qualified, satisfied, terrified, verified, disqualified, dissatisfied, exemplified, identified, insecticide, personified, preoccupied, unsatisfied

-ife   knife, life, strife, wife, housewife, jackknife, nightlife, wildlife

-ific   horrific, Pacific, prolific, specific, terrific, scientific

-ig   big, dig, fig, gig, jig, pig, rig, swig, twig, wig, bigwig, shindig, thingamajig

-igh   high, sigh, thigh

172

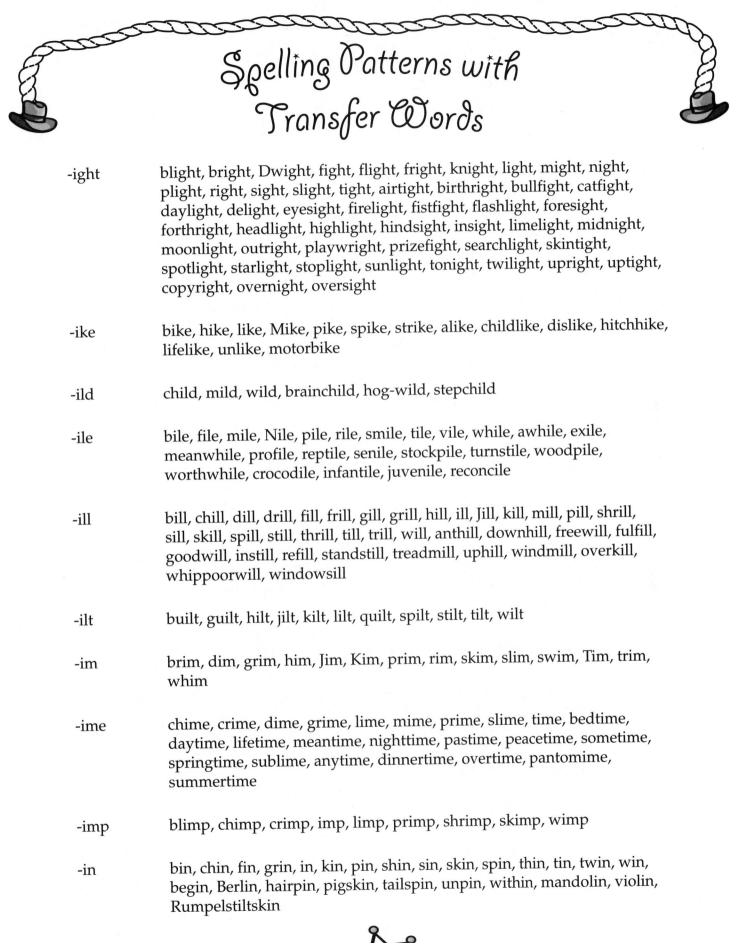

Spelling Patterns with Transfer Words

-ight	blight, bright, Dwight, fight, flight, fright, knight, light, might, night, plight, right, sight, slight, tight, airtight, birthright, bullfight, catfight, daylight, delight, eyesight, firelight, fistfight, flashlight, foresight, forthright, headlight, highlight, hindsight, insight, limelight, midnight, moonlight, outright, playwright, prizefight, searchlight, skintight, spotlight, starlight, stoplight, sunlight, tonight, twilight, upright, uptight, copyright, overnight, oversight
-ike	bike, hike, like, Mike, pike, spike, strike, alike, childlike, dislike, hitchhike, lifelike, unlike, motorbike
-ild	child, mild, wild, brainchild, hog-wild, stepchild
-ile	bile, file, mile, Nile, pile, rile, smile, tile, vile, while, awhile, exile, meanwhile, profile, reptile, senile, stockpile, turnstile, woodpile, worthwhile, crocodile, infantile, juvenile, reconcile
-ill	bill, chill, dill, drill, fill, frill, gill, grill, hill, ill, Jill, kill, mill, pill, shrill, sill, skill, spill, still, thrill, till, trill, will, anthill, downhill, freewill, fulfill, goodwill, instill, refill, standstill, treadmill, uphill, windmill, overkill, whippoorwill, windowsill
-ilt	built, guilt, hilt, jilt, kilt, lilt, quilt, spilt, stilt, tilt, wilt
-im	brim, dim, grim, him, Jim, Kim, prim, rim, skim, slim, swim, Tim, trim, whim
-ime	chime, crime, dime, grime, lime, mime, prime, slime, time, bedtime, daytime, lifetime, meantime, nighttime, pastime, peacetime, sometime, springtime, sublime, anytime, dinnertime, overtime, pantomime, summertime
-imp	blimp, chimp, crimp, imp, limp, primp, shrimp, skimp, wimp
-in	bin, chin, fin, grin, in, kin, pin, shin, sin, skin, spin, thin, tin, twin, win, begin, Berlin, hairpin, pigskin, tailspin, unpin, within, mandolin, violin, Rumpelstiltskin

Spelling Patterns with Transfer Words

-inch   cinch, clinch, finch, flinch, inch, pinch

-ind   1 (as in kind) bind, blind, find, grind, kind, mind, rind, wind, behind, remind, unkind, unwind, colorblind, humankind, mastermind

2 (as in whirlwind) wind, downwind, tailwind, whirlwind, woodwind

-ine   1 (as in dine) dine, fine, line, mine, nine, pine, shine, shrine, spine, swine, twine, vine, whine, wine, airline, alpine, baseline, beeline, canine, clothesline, coastline, combine, confine, deadline, decline, define, divine, entwine, feline, grapevine, guideline, hairline, headline, hemline, incline, lifeline, neckline, outline, outshine, pipeline, recline, refine, shoeshine, sideline, skyline, streamline, sunshine, borderline, intertwine, iodine, Palestine, porcupine, storyline, underline, undermine, valentine

2 (as in routine) Bactine®, chlorine, cuisine, machine, marine, Maxine, ravine, routine, sardine, vaccine, gasoline, guillotine, Josephine, limousine, magazine, Maybelline®, mezzanine, nectarine, quarantine, serpentine, submarine, tambourine, tangerine, trampoline, Vaseline®

-ing   bring, cling, ding, fling, king, ping, ring, sing, sling, spring, sting, string, swing, thing, wing, wring, Beijing, drawstring, earring, offspring, plaything, shoestring, something, anything, everything

-ink   blink, brink, clink, drink, fink, ink, kink, link, mink, pink, rink, shrink, sink, slink, stink, think, wink, hoodwink, rethink

-ip   blip, chip, clip, dip, drip, flip, grip, hip, lip, nip, pip, quip, rip, ship, sip, skip, slip, snip, strip, tip, trip, whip, zip, catnip, courtship, equip, friendship, hardship, kinship, Q-Tip®, spaceship, unzip, battleship, censorship, fellowship, fingertip, internship, leadership, membership, ownership, penmanship, salesmanship, scholarship, sportsmanship, apprenticeship, championship, citizenship, companionship, dictatorship, guardianship

-irt   dirt, flirt, shirt, skirt, squirt, nightshirt, undershirt

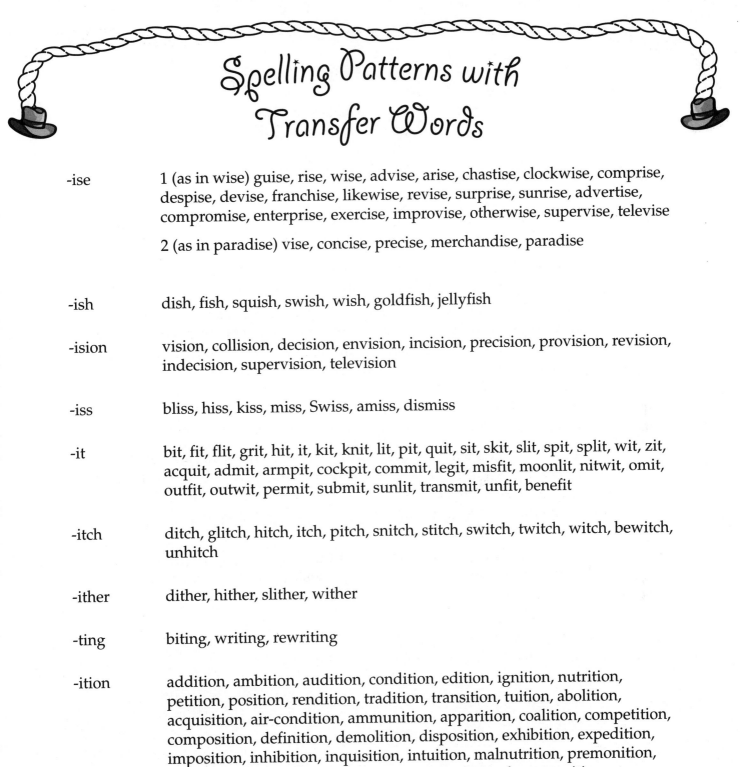

Spelling Patterns with Transfer Words

-ise   1 (as in wise) guise, rise, wise, advise, arise, chastise, clockwise, comprise, despise, devise, franchise, likewise, revise, surprise, sunrise, advertise, compromise, enterprise, exercise, improvise, otherwise, supervise, televise

2 (as in paradise) vise, concise, precise, merchandise, paradise

-ish   dish, fish, squish, swish, wish, goldfish, jellyfish

-ision   vision, collision, decision, envision, incision, precision, provision, revision, indecision, supervision, television

-iss   bliss, hiss, kiss, miss, Swiss, amiss, dismiss

-it   bit, fit, flit, grit, hit, it, kit, knit, lit, pit, quit, sit, skit, slit, spit, split, wit, zit, acquit, admit, armpit, cockpit, commit, legit, misfit, moonlit, nitwit, omit, outfit, outwit, permit, submit, sunlit, transmit, unfit, benefit

-itch   ditch, glitch, hitch, itch, pitch, snitch, stitch, switch, twitch, witch, bewitch, unhitch

-ither   dither, hither, slither, wither

-ting   biting, writing, rewriting

-ition   addition, ambition, audition, condition, edition, ignition, nutrition, petition, position, rendition, tradition, transition, tuition, abolition, acquisition, air-condition, ammunition, apparition, coalition, competition, composition, definition, demolition, disposition, exhibition, expedition, imposition, inhibition, inquisition, intuition, malnutrition, premonition, prohibition, recognition, repetition, superstition, decomposition

-itten   bitten, kitten, mitten, smitten, written, frostbitten, handwritten, typewritten, unwritten

Spelling Patterns with Transfer Words

-ive	1 (as in dive) dive, drive, five, hive, jive, live, strive, thrive, alive, archive, arrive, beehive, connive, contrive, deprive, nosedive, revive, skydive, survive
	2 (as in give) give, live, forgive, outlive, relive
-iver	1 (as in driver) diver, driver, cabdriver, conniver, screwdriver, skydiver
	2 (as in giver) giver, liver, quiver, river, shiver, sliver, deliver, downriver
-iving	living, Thanksgiving
-ix	fix, mix, nix, six, transfix
-o	1 (as in to) do, to, two, who, ado, hairdo, into, misdo, outdo, redo, undo, unto, overdo
	2 (as in go) go, no, pro, so, ago, hello, info, pueblo, Alamo, buffalo, calico, dynamo, Idaho, Mexico, Navajo, Oreo®, radio, ratio, rodeo, Romeo, stereo, studio, Tokyo, video, Geronimo, Pinocchio, pistachio, portfolio
-oast	boast, coast, roast, toast
-oaster	boaster, coaster, roaster, toaster
-oat	bloat, boat, coat, float, gloat, goat, moat, oat, throat, afloat, dreamboat, lifeboat, raincoat, rowboat, scapegoat, steamboat, turncoat, overcoat, petticoat, sugarcoat
-ock	block, clock, crock, dock, flock, jock, knock, lock, mock, rock, shock, smock, sock, stock, deadlock, gridlock, headlock, Hitchcock, livestock, padlock, peacock, roadblock, shamrock, Sherlock, unlock, woodblock, aftershock, laughingstock, poppycock
-og	bog, dog, log, dog, flog, fog, frog, grog, hog, jog, log, bulldog, bullfrog, groundhog, leapfrog, watchdog, catalog, underdog

Spelling Patterns with Transfer Words

-oice   choice, voice, rejoice

-ointment   appointment, disappointment

-oke   broke, choke, Coke®, joke, poke, smoke, spoke, stoke, stroke, woke, awoke, cowpoke, heatstroke, provoke, slowpoke, sunstroke, artichoke

-old   bold, cold, fold, gold, hold, mold, old, scold, sold, told, behold, billfold, blindfold, enfold, foothold, household, retold, stronghold, threshold, unfold, untold, withhold

-ole   dole, hole, mole, pole, role, sole, stole, whole, cajole, console, flagpole, foxhole, keyhole, loophole, manhole, parole, peephole, porthole, pothole, tadpole, buttonhole, camisole, casserole, cubbyhole, pigeonhole

-ome   1 (as in dome) chrome, dome, gnome, home, Rome, syndrome, Astrodome, metronome, palindrome, Superdome

     2 (as in come) come, some, become, outcome, overcome

-ond   blond, bond, fond, pond, beyond, fishpond, respond, correspond, vagabond

-one   1 (as in done) done, none, one, outdone, redone, someone, undone, anyone, everyone, overdone, underdone

     2 (as in bone) bone, clone, cone, drone, hone, lone, phone, prone, shone, stone, throne, tone, zone, alone, backbone, birthstone, condone, cyclone, dethrone, grindstone, headphone, headstone, hormone, jawbone, milestone, outshone, ozone, pinecone, postpone, rhinestone, T-bone, tombstone, trombone, wishbone, baritone, cobblestone, microphone, monotone, saxophone, telephone, xylophone, Yellowstone

-ong   gong, long, song, strong, thong, throng, wrong, along, belong, headlong, headstrong, lifelong, oblong, prolong, sarong, tagalong

Spelling Patterns with Transfer Words

-on't	don't, won't
-oo	boo, goo, moo, too, woo, zoo, ah-choo, bamboo, boo-boo, boohoo, choo-choo, cuckoo, kazoo, shampoo, taboo, tattoo, voodoo, yoo-hoo, ballyhoo, buckaroo, bugaboo, cockatoo, kangaroo, peek-a-boo, switcheroo, Waterloo, hullabaloo, cock-a-doodle-doo
-ood	1 (as in wood) good, hood, stood, wood, childhood, driftwood, redwood, sainthood, brotherhood, fatherhood, Hollywood, likelihood, livelihood, motherhood, neighborhood, sisterhood, understood, misunderstood
	2 (as in food) brood, food, mood, seafood
-oodle	doodle, noodle, poodle
-ook	book, brook, cook, crook, hook, look, nook, rook, shook, took, checkbook, fishhook, handbook, mistook, notebook, outlook, scrapbook, textbook, unhook, overlook
-ool	cool, drool, fool, pool, school, spool, stool, tool, preschool, toadstool, whirlpool, Liverpool
-oom	bloom, boom, broom, doom, gloom, groom, loom, room, zoom, bathroom, bridegroom, classroom, courtroom, heirloom, homeroom, mushroom
-oon	croon, goon, loon, moon, noon, soon, spoon, swoon, baboon, balloon, bassoon, buffoon, cartoon, cocoon, harpoon, lagoon, maroon, monsoon, platoon, pontoon, raccoon, Rangoon, tycoon, typhoon, afternoon, honeymoon, macaroon
-oop	coop, droop, goop, hoop, loop, scoop, snoop, stoop, swoop, troop, whoop
-oor	door, floor, poor, indoor, outdoor, trapdoor

Spelling Patterns with Transfer Words

-oose 1 (as in moose) goose, loose, moose, noose, caboose, footloose, mongoose, papoose, vamoose

2 (as in choose) choose

-op bop, chop, cop, crop, drop, flop, hop, lop, mop, plop, pop, prop, shop, slop, stop, top, Aesop, bebop, bellhop, blacktop, doorstop, eavesdrop, flattop, gumdrop, hilltop, nonstop, pawnshop, raindrop, rooftop, shortstop, teardrop, tiptop, treetop, workshop, barbershop, lollipop, mountaintop

-ope cope, dope, grope, hope, lope, mope, nope, pope, rope, scope, slope, elope, tightrope, towrope, antelope, envelope, horoscope, microscope, periscope, stethoscope, telescope

-ore bore, chore, core, gore, lore, more, pore, snore, score, shore, sore, store, swore, tore, wore, adore, ashore, before, drugstore, encore, explore, eyesore, folklore, galore, ignore, outscore, restore, seashore, therefore, anymore, Baltimore, carnivore, evermore, furthermore, nevermore, Singapore, sophomore, Theodore, underscore, forevermore

-orn born, corn, horn, morn, scorn, sworn, thorn, torn, worn, acorn, adorn, bullhorn, foghorn, forlorn, greenhorn, inborn, lovelorn, newborn, outworn, popcorn, reborn, shoehorn, timeworn, unborn, Capricorn, unicorn, weatherworn

-ort fort, port, short, snort, sort, sport, airport, cavort, cohort, contort, deport, distort, escort, export, import, Newport, passport, report, resort, seaport, spoilsport, support, transport

-ose chose, close, hose, nose, pose, prose, rose, those, dispose, enclose, expose, impose, oppose, propose, suppose, decompose, overexpose

-ost 1 (as in post) ghost, host, most, post, almost, bedpost, goalpost, guidepost, outpost, signpost, topmost, utmost, innermost

2 (as in cost) cost, frost, lost, defrost

Spelling Patterns with Transfer Words

-ot   blot, clot, cot, dot, got, hot, jot, knot, lot, not, plot, pot, rot, Scot, shot, slot, snot, spot, tot, trot, cannot, forgot, inkblot, jackpot, mascot, robot, slingshot, snapshot, teapot, whatnot, apricot, Camelot, flowerpot, Lancelot

-ote   note, quote, tote, vote, wrote, devote, footnote, keynote, misquote, outvote, promote, remote, rewrote, anecdote, antidote

-other   brother, mother, other, smother, another, godmother, grandmother, stepmother

-otion   lotion, motion, notion, potion, commotion, devotion, emotion, promotion, locomotion

-otter   hotter, otter, plotter, potter, totter, trotter, globetrotter, teeter-totter

-ouch   couch, crouch, grouch, ouch, pouch, slouch, vouch

-oud   cloud, loud, proud, shroud, aloud, thundercloud

-ould   could, should, would

-ound   bound, found, ground, hound, mound, pound, round, sound, wound, abound, around, astound, background, bloodhound, campground, compound, dumbfound, earthbound, foreground, greyhound, inbound, newfound, outbound, playground, profound, rebound, snowbound, spellbound, surround, battleground, runaround, underground

-ount   count, mount, account, amount, discount, paramount, tantamount

-ouse   blouse, douse, house, louse, mouse, spouse, clubhouse, courthouse, doghouse, firehouse, lighthouse, outhouse, penthouse, roughhouse, warehouse

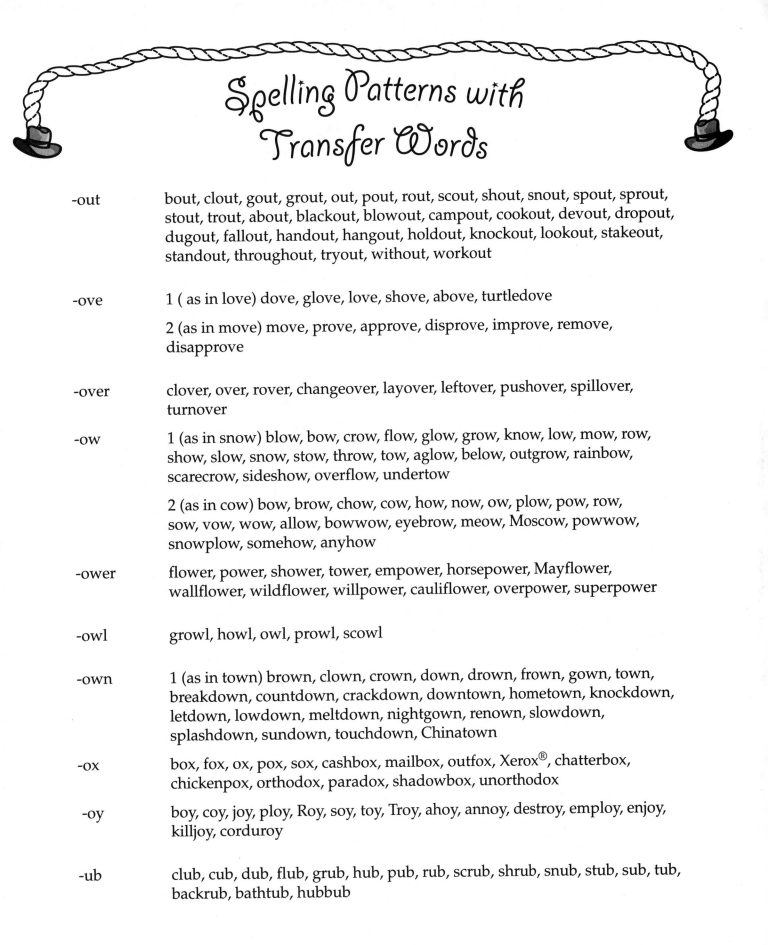

Spelling Patterns with Transfer Words

-out   bout, clout, gout, grout, out, pout, rout, scout, shout, snout, spout, sprout, stout, trout, about, blackout, blowout, campout, cookout, devout, dropout, dugout, fallout, handout, hangout, holdout, knockout, lookout, stakeout, standout, throughout, tryout, without, workout

-ove   1 (as in love) dove, glove, love, shove, above, turtledove

2 (as in move) move, prove, approve, disprove, improve, remove, disapprove

-over   clover, over, rover, changeover, layover, leftover, pushover, spillover, turnover

-ow   1 (as in snow) blow, bow, crow, flow, glow, grow, know, low, mow, row, show, slow, snow, stow, throw, tow, aglow, below, outgrow, rainbow, scarecrow, sideshow, overflow, undertow

2 (as in cow) bow, brow, chow, cow, how, now, ow, plow, pow, row, sow, vow, wow, allow, bowwow, eyebrow, meow, Moscow, powwow, snowplow, somehow, anyhow

-ower   flower, power, shower, tower, empower, horsepower, Mayflower, wallflower, wildflower, willpower, cauliflower, overpower, superpower

-owl   growl, howl, owl, prowl, scowl

-own   1 (as in town) brown, clown, crown, down, drown, frown, gown, town, breakdown, countdown, crackdown, downtown, hometown, knockdown, letdown, lowdown, meltdown, nightgown, renown, slowdown, splashdown, sundown, touchdown, Chinatown

-ox   box, fox, ox, pox, sox, cashbox, mailbox, outfox, Xerox®, chatterbox, chickenpox, orthodox, paradox, shadowbox, unorthodox

-oy   boy, coy, joy, ploy, Roy, soy, toy, Troy, ahoy, annoy, destroy, employ, enjoy, killjoy, corduroy

-ub   club, cub, dub, flub, grub, hub, pub, rub, scrub, shrub, snub, stub, sub, tub, backrub, bathtub, hubbub

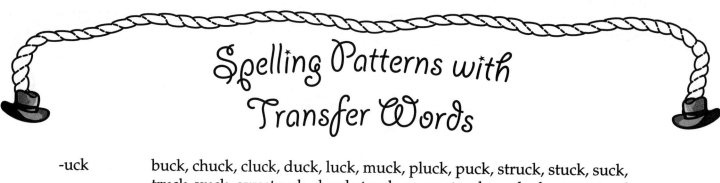

Spelling Patterns with Transfer Words

-uck	buck, chuck, cluck, duck, luck, muck, pluck, puck, struck, stuck, suck, truck, yuck, awestruck, dumbstruck, moonstruck, potluck, stagestruck, starstruck, woodchuck, thunderstruck
-ucky	ducky, lucky, mucky, plucky, yucky, Kentucky, unlucky
-uddle	cuddle, huddle, muddle, puddle, befuddle
-ue	blue, clue, cue, due, glue, hue, rue, sue, true, construe, miscue, pursue, revue, subdue, untrue, avenue, misconstrue, overdue, residue, revenue
-uff	bluff, buff, cuff, fluff, gruff, huff, muff, puff, scruff, scuff, snuff, stuff, handcuff, rebuff, overstuff
-ug	bug, chug, drug, dug, hug, jug, lug, mug, plug, pug, rug, shrug, slug, smug, snug, thug, tug, bedbug, earplug, humbug, unplug, jitterbug, ladybug, litterbug
-uilt	built, guilt, quilt, rebuilt
-um	bum, chum, drum, glum, gum, hum, mum, plum, scum, slum, strum, sum, yum, eardrum, humdrum, chrysanthemum
-umber	lumber, number, slumber, cucumber, outnumber
-umble	crumble, fumble, grumble, humble, jumble, mumble, rumble, stumble, tumble
-ummer	bummer, drummer, hummer, strummer, summer, midsummer
-ummy	chummy, crummy, dummy, gummy, mummy, rummy, scummy, tummy, yummy
-ump	bump, chump, clump, dump, grump, hump, jump, lump, plump, pump, rump, slump, stump, thump, trump, ump

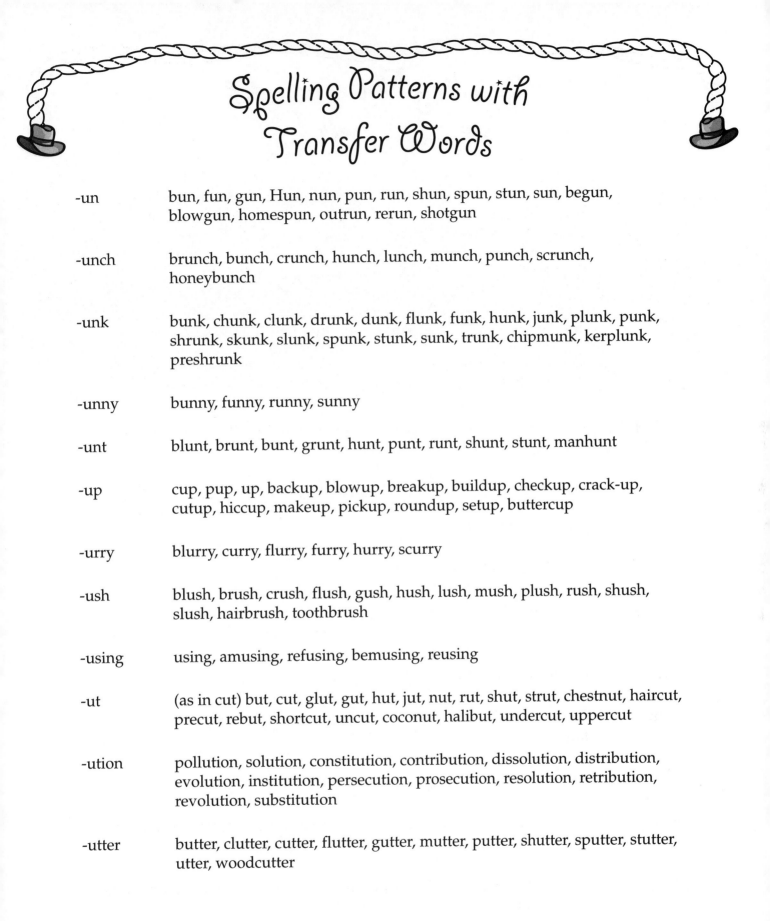

Spelling Patterns with Transfer Words

-un	bun, fun, gun, Hun, nun, pun, run, shun, spun, stun, sun, begun, blowgun, homespun, outrun, rerun, shotgun
-unch	brunch, bunch, crunch, hunch, lunch, munch, punch, scrunch, honeybunch
-unk	bunk, chunk, clunk, drunk, dunk, flunk, funk, hunk, junk, plunk, punk, shrunk, skunk, slunk, spunk, stunk, sunk, trunk, chipmunk, kerplunk, preshrunk
-unny	bunny, funny, runny, sunny
-unt	blunt, brunt, bunt, grunt, hunt, punt, runt, shunt, stunt, manhunt
-up	cup, pup, up, backup, blowup, breakup, buildup, checkup, crack-up, cutup, hiccup, makeup, pickup, roundup, setup, buttercup
-urry	blurry, curry, flurry, furry, hurry, scurry
-ush	blush, brush, crush, flush, gush, hush, lush, mush, plush, rush, shush, slush, hairbrush, toothbrush
-using	using, amusing, refusing, bemusing, reusing
-ut	(as in cut) but, cut, glut, gut, hut, jut, nut, rut, shut, strut, chestnut, haircut, precut, rebut, shortcut, uncut, coconut, halibut, undercut, uppercut
-ution	pollution, solution, constitution, contribution, dissolution, distribution, evolution, institution, persecution, prosecution, resolution, retribution, revolution, substitution
-utter	butter, clutter, cutter, flutter, gutter, mutter, putter, shutter, sputter, stutter, utter, woodcutter

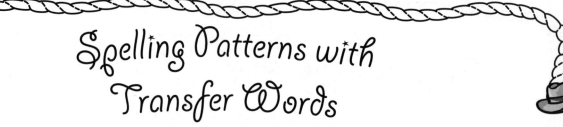

Spelling Patterns with Transfer Words

-y   by, cry, dry, fly, fry, guy, my, pry, shy, sky, sly, spry, spy, sty, try, why, wry, ally, apply, comply, defy, deny, firefly, horsefly, imply, July, nearby, outcry, pigsty, rely, reply, standby, supply, amplify, beautify, butterfly, certify, clarify, classify, dignify, dragonfly, falsify, fortify, glorify, gratify, horrify, hushaby, justify, lullaby, magnify, modify, mortify, multiply, mummify, mystify, notify, nullify, occupy, pacify, passerby, petrify, purify, qualify, ratify, rectify, satisfy, signify, simplify, specify, terrify, testify, unify, verify, disqualify, dissatisfy, electrify, exemplify, identify, intensify, preoccupy, solidify

Rounding Up The Rhymes

Lesson Plan Reproducible

Title _____

1. Read the book for students' enjoyment and understanding. (Self Selected Reading, Guided Reading, or content area)
2. Decide how much of the text you will use for this activity (entire book or specific pages). If you are only revisiting specific pages, mark the pages to be used.
3. During Working with Words, reread the pages you've marked, having students listen for and identify the rhyming words.
4. As you are reading, write the rhyming words that children identify on index cards and display them in a pocket chart (or write them on a piece of chart paper).
5. Have students consider each set of rhyming words. Keep rhyming words with the same spelling patterns. Discard rhyming words that are not spelled alike.
6. Transfer/extend the spelling patterns of the rhyming words you keep to new words to read/write.

Rhymes to keep

_____ _____
_____ _____
_____ _____
_____ _____
_____ _____
_____ _____
_____ _____
_____ _____

Rhymes to discard

_____ _____
_____ _____
_____ _____
_____ _____
_____ _____
_____ _____
_____ _____
_____ _____

Words to extend/transfer for each spelling pattern

_____ _____ _____ _____
_____ _____ _____ _____
_____ _____ _____ _____
_____ _____ _____ _____
_____ _____ _____ _____
_____ _____ _____ _____
_____ _____ _____ _____

Curriculum Support Sample

Focused Pattern	Book Used	Standard Covered	Date Introduced Reviewed Assessed
ack	The Rules	1.A1.a.	**I** 9-3 **R** 9-5 **A** 9-9
un	Skittles® Riddles Math	1.A1.a.	**I** 9-10 **R** 9-12 **A** 9-16
o (long)	I Love Words	1.A1.a.	**I** 9-17 **R** 9-19 **A** 9-23
og	My Little Sister Ate One Hare	1.A1.a.	**I** 9-24 **R** 9-26 **A** 9-30
ail	House Mouse Senate Mouse	1.A1.a.	**I** 10-1 **R** 10-3 **A** 10-7
ar	Miss Spider's New Car	1.A1.a.	**I** 10-8 **R** 10-10 **A** 10-14
aw	Rumble in the Jungle	1.A1.a.	**I** 10-15 **R** 10-16 **A** 10-18
eed	Belly Button Boy	1.A1.a.	**I** 10-22 **R** 10-24 **A** 10-29
ix	Somewhere in the Ocean	1.A1.a.	**I** 11-5 **R** 11-7 **A** 11-11
old	Birds Build Nests	1.A1.a.	**I** 11-12 **R** 11-14 **A** 11-18
oo	Put Me in the Zoo	1.A1.a.	**I** 11-19 **R** 11-21 **A** 11-25
ort	If I Ran the Rain Forest	1.A1.a.	**I** 12-3 **R** 12-5 **A** 12-9
um	Hello School!	1.A1.a.	**I** 12-10 **R** 12-12 **A** 12-16

Curriculum Support Reproducible

Focused Pattern	Book Used	Standard Covered	Date Introduced Reviewed Assessed
			I R A
			I R A
			I R A
			I R A
			I R A
			I R A
			I R A
			I R A
			I R A
			I R A
			I R A
			I R A

Children's Books Cited

The 10 Best Things About My Dad by Christine Loomis (Scholastic Paperbacks, 2004)

Angel Pig and the Hidden Christmas by Jan L. Waldron (Puffin Books, 2000)

The Bear Came Over to My House by Rick Walton (Puffin Books, 2003)

Bear Wants More by Karma Wilson (Margaret K. McElderry Books, 2003)

Belly Button Boy by Peter Maloney and Felicia Zekauskas (Puffin Books, 2003)

The Best Vacation Ever by Stuart J. Murphy (HarperTrophy, 1997)

Birds Build Nests by Yvonne Winer (Charlesbridge Publishing, 2002)

The Brand New Kid by Katie Couric (Doubleday, 2000)

Butterflies Fly by Yvonne Winer (Charlesbridge Publishing, 2001)

Counting Is for the Birds by Frank Mazzola, Jr. (Charlesbridge Publishing, 1997)

The Crayon Box that Talked by Shane DeRolf (Random House Books for Young Readers, 1997)

Don't Call Me Pig: A Javelina Story by Conrad J. Storad (RGU Group, 1999)

Each Peach Pear Plum by Janet and Allan Ahlberg (Puffin Books, 1986)

The Flea's Sneeze by Lynn Downey (Henry Holt and Co., 2000)

Follow Me! by Bethany Roberts (Clarion Books, 1998)

Get Up and Go! by Stuart J. Murphy (HarperTrophy, 1996)

Giraffes Can't Dance by Giles Andreae (Scholastic, 2001)

Goodnight Moon by Margaret Wise Brown (HarperTrophy, 1977)

Green Wilma by Tedd Arnold (Puffin Books, 1998)

The Grumpy Morning by Pamela Duncan Edwards (Hyperion, 1998)

Hello School! A Classroom Full of Poems by Dee Lillegard (Dragonfly Books, 2003)

Hooray for You!: A Celebration of You-ness by Marianne Richmond (Marianne Richmond Studios, Inc., 2001)

House Mouse, Senate Mouse by Peter W. and Cheryl Shaw Barnes (Rosebud Books, 1996)

How I Spent My Summer Vacation by Mark Teague (Dragonfly Books, 1997)

How Many, How Many, How Many by Rick Walton (Candlewick Press, 1996)

I Love Words by Barbara Barbieri McGrath (Charlesbridge Publishing, 2003)

I Love You Because You're You by Liza Baker (Cartwheel Books, 2001)

I Love You, Mom by Iris Hiskey Arno (Troll Communications, 2000)

If I Ran the Rain Forest: All About Tropical Rain Forests by Bonnie Worth (Random House Books for Young Readers, 2003)

If the Shoe Fits by Alison Jackson (Henry Holt and Co., 2001)

I'll Teach My Dog 100 Words by Michael Frith (HarperCollins, 1983)

In 1492 by Jean Marzollo (Scholastic, 1993)

Inchworm and a Half by Elinor J. Pinczes (Houghton Mifflin, 2003)

Itchy, Itchy Chicken Pox by Grace MacCarone (Scholastic, 1992)

It's St. Patrick's Day! by Rebecca Gomez (Cartwheel Books, 2004)

Jennifer Jones Won't Leave Me Alone by Frieda Wishinsky (HaperCollins, 1997)

The Library by Sarah Stewart (Farrar, Straus and Giroux, 1999)

Little Miss Spider by David Kirk (Scholastic Press, 2003)

Lizards for Lunch: A Roadrunner's Tale by Conrad J. Storad (RGU Group, 2002)

Loud Lips Lucy by Tolya L. Thompson (Savor Publishing House, 2001)

The M&M's® Brand Color Pattern Book by Barbara Barbieri McGrath (Charlesbridge Publishing, 2002)

The M&M's® Brand Counting Book by Barbara Barbieri McGrath (Charlesbridge Publishing, 1994)

Many Luscious Lollipops: A Book about Adjectives by Ruth Heller (Putnam Publishing Group, 1998)

Marshall, the Courthouse Mouse: A Tail of the U.S. Supreme Court by Peter W. and Cheryl Shaw Barnes (Rosebud Books, 1998)

A Mink, a Fink, a Skating Rink: What Is a Noun? by Brian P. Cleary (Carolrhoda Books, Inc., 1999)

Miss Spider's New Car by David Kirk (Scholastic Press, 1997)

More M&M's® Brand Math by Barbara Barbieri McGrath (Charlesbridge Publishing, 1998)

More Parts by Tedd Arnold (Puffin Books, 2003)

Motherlove by Virginia Kroll (Dawn Publications, 1998)

The Mouse Before Christmas by Michael Garland (Puffin Books, 2001)

Mr. Monopoly's Amusement Park: A Math Adventure by Jackie Glassman (Scholastic, 2001)

Mr. Wiggle's Book by Paula Craig (Instructional Fair, 2001)

My Daddy and I by P. K. Hallinan (Candy Cane Press, 2002)

My Grandpa and I by P. K. Hallinan (Candy Cane Press, 2002)

My Hippie Grandmother by Reeve Lindbergh (Candlewick Press, 2003)

My Little Sister Ate One Hare by Bill Grossman (Dragonfly Books, 1998)

Mystery Mansion by Michael Garland (Puffin Books, 2003)

The Night Before Easter by Natasha Wing (Grosset and Dunlap, 1999)

The Night Before Kindergarten by Natasha Wing (Grosset and Dunlap, 2001)

The Night Before the Night Before Christmas by Natasha Wing (Grosset and Dunlap, 2002)

The Night Before Summer Vacation by Natasha Wing (Grosset and Dunlap, 2002)

The Night Before the Tooth Fairy by Natasha Wing (Grosset and Dunlap, 2003)

The Night Before Valentine's Day by Natasha Wing (Grosset and Dunlap, 2000)

Oh, How I Wished I Could Read! by John Gile (John Gile Communications, 1995)

Over in the Garden by Jennifer Ward (Rising Moon Books, 2002)

Over in the Meadow: A Counting Rhyme by Olive A. Wadsworth (North-South Books, 2002)

Parts by Tedd Arnold (Puffin Books, 2000)

Put Me in the Zoo by Robert Lopshire (Random House Books for Young Readers, 1960)

Quick as a Cricket by Audrey Wood (Child's Play International, Ltd., 1990)

Rabbit's Pajama Party by Stuart J. Murphy (HarperTrophy, 1999)

A Rainbow of Friends by P. K. Hallinan (Ideals Publications, 2002)

The Rules by Marty Kelley (Knowledge Unlimited, 2000)

Rumble in the Jungle by Giles Andreae (Tiger Tales, 2001)

The Shape of Things by Dayle Ann Dodds (Candlewick Press, 1996)

Skittles® Riddles Math by Barbara Barbieri McGrath (Charlesbridge Publishing, 2001)

Sleepless Beauty by Frances Minters (Puffin Books, 1999)

Somewhere in the Ocean by Jennifer Ward and T. J. Marsh (Rising Moon Books, 2000)

Summer Stinks by Marty Kelley (Zino Press Children's Books, 2001)

The Thingumajig Book of Manners by Irene Keller (Ideals Children's Books, 2001)

This Is the Sea that Feeds Us by Robert F. Baldwin (Dawn Publications, 1998)

This Is the Way We Go to School by Edith Baer (Scholastic, 1992)

Today Is Thanksgiving by P. K. Hallinan (Ideals Publications, 2001)

'Twas the Day AFTER Thanksgiving by Mavis Smith (Little Simon, 2002)

'Twas the Night Before Thanksgiving by Dav Pilkey (Scholastic, 2004)

The Way I Feel by Janan Cain (Parenting Press, 2000)

The Wedding by Eve Bunting (Charlesbridge Publishing, 2003)

Where Once There Was a Wood by Denise Fleming (Henry Holt and Co., 2000)

Wild About Books by Judy Sierra (Knopf Books for Young Readers, 2004)

The Wolf's Story by Brenda Parkes (Rigby, 2000)

Woodrow, the White House Mouse by Peter W. and Cheryl Shaw Barnes (Scholastic, 2000)

Worry Wart Wes by Tolya L. Thompson (Savor Publishing, 2002)

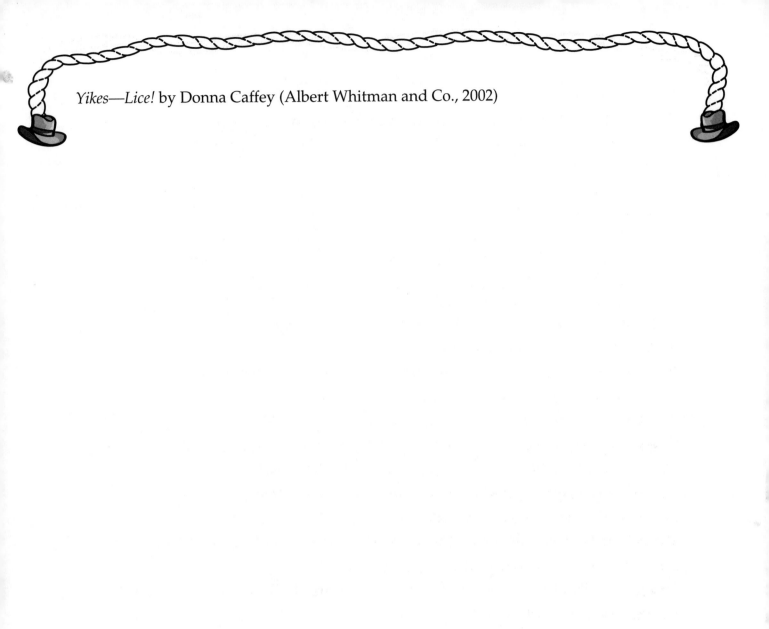

Yikes—Lice! by Donna Caffey (Albert Whitman and Co., 2002)

Professional References

Cunningham, P. M. and Hall, D. P. (1997). *Month-by-Month Phonics for First Grade*. Greensboro, NC: Carson-Dellosa.

Cunningham, P. M. and Hall, D. P. (1997). *Month-by-Month Phonics for Upper Grades*. Greensboro, NC: Carson-Dellosa.

Cunningham, P. M. and Hall, D. P. (1998). *Month-by-Month Phonics for Third Grade*. Greensboro, NC: Carson-Dellosa.

Cunningham, P. M., Hall, D. P., and Sigmon, C. M. (1999). *The Teacher's Guide to the Four Blocks*®. Greensboro, NC: Carson-Dellosa.

Cunningham, P. M., Hall, D. P., and Cunningham, J. W. (2000). *Guided Reading the Four-Blocks*® *Way*. Greensboro, NC: Carson-Dellosa.

Cunningham, P. M., Hall, D. P., and Gambrell, L. B. (2002). *Self-Selected Reading the Four-Blocks*® *Way*. Greensboro, NC: Carson-Dellosa.

Cunningham, P. M., Moore, S. A., Cunningham, J. W., and Moore, D. W. (2004). *Reading and Writing in Elementary Classrooms: Research-Based K–4 Instruction*. Allyn and Bacon.

Hall, D. P. and Cunningham, P. M. (1998). *Month-by-Month Phonics for Second Grade*. Greensboro, NC: Carson-Dellosa.